# GOd

## HAS THE

# Final Word

ROBERT GERMROTH
AND
MAURICIO CRESPO

Trilogy Christian Publishers
A Wholly Owned Subsidiary of Trinity Broadcasting Network
2442 Michelle Drive
Tustin, CA 92780

Cover design by: Cornerstone Creative Solutions

For information, address Trilogy Christian Publishing
Rights Department, 2442 Michelle Drive, Tustin, Ca 92780.
Trilogy Christian Publishing/ TBN and colophon are trademarks of Trinity
Broadcasting Network.

For information about special discounts for bulk purchases, please contact
Trilogy Christian Publishing.

Manufactured in the United States of America

Trilogy Disclaimer: The views and content expressed in this book are those of
the author and may not necessarily reflect the views and doctrine of Trilogy
Christian Publishing or the Trinity Broadcasting Network.

10 9 8 7 6 5 4 3 2 1

Library of Congress Cataloging-in-Publication Data is available.

ISBN 978-1-64773-865-5 (Print Book)
ISBN 978-1-64773-866-2 (ebook)

# Endorsements

The first time I heard Robert's testimony, I was impressed with his faith and his miraculous healing. Today, after reading *God Has the Final Word* and knowing the details of Robert's last days on earth, I was able to reaffirm that the most powerful miracle that God bestows on us will always be the salvation of man.

There is something in each of us that tells us we were created for a greater purpose. During Robert Germroth's funeral, seven persons gave their lives to the Lord. He is surely rejoicing that with his passing, seven became alive and received the assurance of heaven and with that, the miracle of salvation.

—*Rev. Alberto M. Delgado, MA, DM, ThD,
Senior Pastor, Alpha and Omega Church*

To everyone that has faced the monster of cancer, who has fought, bled, and struggled, and to their families along for the ride. This book is for you. God knows your pain, and He knows your victory. The battle is His. Fight on.

To Dad.

I have been crucified with Christ; it is no longer I who live, but Christ lives in me; and the *life* which I now live in the flesh I live by faith in the Son of God, who loved me and gave Himself for me.

—Galatians 2:20 (NKJV)

# Contents

# Foreword

Our daughter Alicia was always fascinated and wanted to hear the story of how Robert and I met, dated, fell in love, got engaged, and got married in seven months. We knew early on in our relationship that we loved and trusted each other. Our first marriages both ended in divorce, and we shared the pain of our spouses leaving us for someone else. So our union was one of promises, love, and trust. It was not an easy start since ours was a blended family with my two little ones and his one son. We raised them all together in our home, knowing the importance of the Word of God. The Bible and its verses were always topics of conversation and discussions, especially at dinnertime.

Naturally, when Robert was diagnosed with stage 4 lung cancer, we immediately turned to our faith and the comfort of God's Word. Healing scriptures on sticky notes were placed all over the house to remind us of His promises. I've always been amazed how God created the world and put it all in motion. He could have done anything He wanted— yet He gave us free will to love, to know, and to choose Him. Every word in the Bible gives us specific instructions to live a happy, fruitful, and successful life. Somehow, that message does not reach everyone, and people go through life never opening the book or knowing what it says. The Bible is a love letter from our heavenly Father with promises and blessings.

It's that book that I clung to during the entire process of Robert's treatments and doctor visits. I would read it out loud to him during his hospital stays, or we would read together silently after dinner and share our thoughts afterward. It was that book that helped me when I felt frozen with fear before we heard the results of a CT scan or MRI. Robert was more knowledgeable in the Word of God since he had attended Bible study classes before we met. He was the one who guided our family discussions and answered our questions during dinnertime. It was Robert who led our family and friends once a month at our home for a faith-group gathering and Bible lesson. It was him who taught our kids that the only way to heaven was through a relationship with Jesus Christ.

Some people begin to seek God when a tragedy or difficult time occurs in their lives. Although that is the best answer to any problem, God can begin to bless you now when all is good. Building a relationship with God takes time, and it's good to know that He is there any time you need Him. I can't imagine how I would get through those first six months of Robert's chemo treatments and radiation not having the peace of God and knowing that He was listening to my daily, and sometimes hourly, prayers.

There's no better gift that you can give to your children, your spouse, and yourself than the knowledge of Jesus's love and why He died on the cross. Give them the Word of God that gives peace beyond all understanding during the most painful circumstances and worship together as a family. They will know that they are never alone and God is always listening. The most difficult lesson to learn and understand is that God hears all our prayers and His answer is always yes and amen. Yet the answer may not come when we want it or how we expect it to come. His thoughts and plans are bigger and better than ours, and God alone has the final word.

I believe God allowed us to go through what we went through to remind us that our sole focus is a relationship with Him. The storms of life showed up, but so did He! And even when we go through the hardest things imaginable and we wonder why and the answer doesn't come, He is still there— sitting with us in the silence. And He, and only He, can look at an impossible situation and make good come out of it.

Never let go of Him,
Leila Germroth

# Just a Cough

*Maury*

"Weddings are a new beginning," I told the bride and groom. "It's the end of your lives as individuals, starting together a new life as one."

In their parents' backyard, with the sunset behind us, I pronounced my closest friends man and wife. The crowd behind them stood and cheered as they kissed. She was in that crowd, and throughout the ceremony, between the bride and groom, I stole glances to see her. The evening sun bounced off her long strawberry-blond hair, bringing out her eyes. And to my surprise, they were staring back at me. Music started playing, and while the best man and maid of honor did their speeches, I sat next to her, my arm around her shoulder.

"Not bad for a first time, right?"

"One could say you've done this before!"

"One would be wrong…"

"You did almost call the bride a different name, so there's that."

"I really don't like you right now, you know that, right?"

"So there's no sixth date, then?" she asked, laughing.

"Shut up!"

We had our first date five days ago, and we saw each other every night since—going out for coffee, for gnocchi at an Italian restaurant, and sitting on her parents' porch, it didn't matter. We were together. And I was terrified of screwing it up.

After the speeches, the caterer opened the buffet and guests crowded around it. I made the line for the food while she went to the bar. Trays of ham croquettes, Caesar salad, and a forest paella, with pork and chicken instead of chicken, were being spooned onto plates.

"Here." She handed me a glass with bourbon swirling in ice. "An old-fashioned, right? I noticed you ordered that the other day."

"You know," I said, squeezing her hand tight, "I really, really like you."

"I spoke to my mom about it, and I hope it doesn't freak you out, but when you know, you know. I love you."

"Oh, thank God!" I laughed, taking a swig of bourbon. "I love you too!"

"I figured, but you know what this means, right?"

"What?"

"I said it first! Ha!" She pulled away and grabbed a plate. "Oooh, croquetas!"

Before we could officially be a couple, I had one major obstacle to overcome—her dad's approval. He was an old-fashioned South Carolina country boy whose idea of settling differences involved fists behind a woodshed, and carried a pocketknife everywhere he went.

"What do your parents like to eat?" I asked, cutting a piece of wedding cake with my fork.

"Seafood, shrimp or fish," she said between mouthfuls. "And rice! My mom loves coconut rice! What are you thinking?"

"I'm thinking dinner, all four of us, then we have a chance to talk." I poured a little bourbon from my drink on the cake, soaking it.

"That go—what are you doing to that cake!"

"Making it taste better!"

"You're so weird!"

"Doesn't matter! You looooove me!" I said, leaning in for a kiss on her cheek.

We tried for that weekend before I left, but her dad had bronchitis and needed to recover. Two weeks later, I was back in Miami, and this time I was determined to get his approval, even if I had to ply him with chicken soup between words. By the grace of God, he felt better, and that Saturday I cooked dinner at their house.

"So! Alicia said you wanted to talk to me?" Robert said after dinner. "Let's go into the backyard, where we can talk in peace." She eyed me nervously as we got up.

Leila and Alicia stayed behind, cleaning up leftover plates of mushroom risotto, grilled peach salad, and snapper into plastic containers. I followed Robert out to the backyard, by the pool; we sat on wicker chairs facing each other.

"Why do you want to date my daughter?" Robert asked, stifling a cough. "You should know, she's special. She's just like her mother. She can be difficult, gullible, and so stubborn! But she has such a good heart." He laughed.

"Robert, we first met two years ago at a friend's house for Thanksgiving. Immediately I noticed her. She was the prettiest girl there. She sat next to my mom, and they talked like friends all night. That was important to me."

Robert smiled, leaning forward, resting his elbows on his knees to hear me better.

"I had a girlfriend at that time, and she told our mutual friends I wasn't her type to avoid getting between me and my then girlfriend. I know the kind of woman she is. One with the same integrity raised me. And I've never found that with anyone else." I leaned forward too, locking eyes with him. "That's why I want your permission to date her. I've never asked a father's permission before, but I know this is the right thing to do."

Muffled behind the door, I could hear plates clattering in the sink, and the muted voices inside likely talking about how it was going.

"Alicia told me you believe in God and you're spirit filled. That's good." Robert coughed. "She told me you've read the Bible, and I can tell you go to a church filled with the Holy Spirit. Back in Charleston, I was also in a spirit-filled church. When I was a member of their board of directors, we asked everyone in the Bible classes one question: What is God? Everybody would write these long paragraphs. Just pages and pages on the subject, how God is everywhere, how He can do anything, how Jesus is God, etc. But very, *very* few people—I can count them with one hand—had a clear answer. So tell me now, what is God?"

*No pressure!*

"Did you really not like the dinner?" I asked, laughing. "I should have made you shrimp instead of the fish!"

He slapped his thigh and giggled, but a raspy, dry cough interrupted it. His blue eyes turned watery from the sting in his throat. He sat there in silence, looking into my eyes, unblinking, waiting for my answer.

"God is love. He starts there, I think," I said.

"Love"—*cough cough*—"that's right! That's what it all comes down to. No matter what you do, no matter where you get in life, you will never be able to outrun God's love. Remember that." He smiled, lines forming at the corner of his eyes. "You did it right in talking to me first. But I just have to say, just be sure. There are a lot of young bucks out there trying to play around and sow their wild oats. I don't want that for my daughter. So just be sure. She's very trusting and gets easily attached. Just be sure!"

I leaned forward to meet his eyes, interlocking my fingers in my hands. "I am sure. One day I'd like to marry her."

"We'll see!" He laughed. "Don't get too carried away just yet. I'm going to give you my blessing to date my daughter, but you have to promise me one thing! See, it's a joke that I've been playing on Alicia since she was a little girl. I always told her that the man I would allow to marry her would have to promise, dead-set, pinky-swear promise"—he slapped his hand on his thigh with every word, really driving the point home—"to name the firstborn son Robert Germroth. That way, she can carry my name to the next generation too. All you have to do is go with it! Oooh, she'll be so mad!" He stomped his feet, laughing in excitement. "Let's go back inside." I followed him back to the living room; the back of his shirt read, "Ten Rules for Dating My Daughter."

Leila and Alicia had washed, dried, swept, and vacuumed every inch of the kitchen by the time we walked in. Crumpled paper towels with orange blots were the only evidence that risotto had been cooked in that kitchen.

"Did you get it?" asked Alicia, wide-eyed, her cheeks flushed from anxiety. "Tell me you got it!" She handed Robert and me bowls with hazelnut mousse. "Oh god, nobody is saying anything!"

"Are you trying to bribe me with sugar?" I asked, scooping a bite of the mousse.

"Yes! Would that help? Yes!"

I could hear Robert coughing in the background as he settled into his armchair. "Why don't you ask him?"

"Spapi! Well?"

21

Robert had never approved of any of her past boy-friends, so this was new territory for all of us. None of them ever asked for permission either.

He slowly ate the mousse, savoring her anticipation more than the chocolate, holding back giggles as she paced back and forth in front of his chair. "I'll allow it."

"Yesss!" She threw her arms in the air. "Oh my god, yay!"

"Time out!" He whistled, holding up his hands into a T shape. "He's already given me his word to name your first kid after me! That was the deal!" He waved his finger at me. "And remember, you're only as good as your word!"

"What? No way! Did you seriously agree to that!?"

"I'm afraid so. Our first kid will have to be named Robert Germroth Crespo," I said, meeting her eyes.

"What if it's a girl?"

"Especially if it's a girl, poor kid! But a deal is a deal!"

"Mommy! Talk some sense into Spapi!"

Robert and I stole glances at each other while she ran to her mother for support, trying to stifle the laughter building in our throats.

"You were right, gullible! By the way, Robert, how long have you had that cough?" I asked, sitting on the couch next to him.

"It's been a while," he said. "At first I thought it was bronchitis. My general practitioner gave me medication to take for ten days, and *nothing*, man. Now he says its pneumonia. Can you believe it? I have to take more medication for ten more days to clear it up. If that doesn't work, he's sending me to a pulmonologist to see what's going on with my lungs."

"Do you feel bad?" I asked, finishing the last of the dessert.

"No. Just really tired lately. Can you believe this, man?" he asked again. "First bronchitis, and now pneumonia."

\*\*\*\*\*

Driving out of Miami always feels like the moment a plane takes off on the runway. As you accelerate, the noise, congestion, traffic, and grime of the city get left behind. In their place, you feel space, the open, uncluttered space, where you can breathe a little easier and see more blue sky.

Alicia wouldn't let go of me the night before, when I went to their house to say goodbye.

"It's only two weeks," I said. "I'll be back soon!"

"It's two whole weeks! Basically forever!"

"We'll talk every night."

"I know."

Farms and open fields flanked the road, cows took shade under oak trees at the edges of the fields, finding refuge from the tropical sun. My car roared past them, causing them to raise their heads in alarm. I left Miami behind, my now-married friends, and my new girlfriend, turning my thoughts to Jacksonville and life with my mom.

For as long as I could remember, life was just the three of us: my mom, my brother, and I. She stood firm in God when my father walked out. Being a single mother, she was no stranger to impossible circumstances, and through that faith, she brought my brother and me from Cuba, through Costa Rica, and finally to Miami.

While my brother and I were in school, she would work three jobs to pay for the rent, put food on the table, and teach my brother and me how to be men, despite the fact that none of us had a father figure to draw from. Growing up, we didn't have much, but even in the face of that, she drove into my brother and me the importance of a relationship with God. "In this life, you only have God and each other," she would tell us. "And even when the world fails you, God will never fail you." So we grew up knowing that terrible things could happen, but God was always there, in those terrible things too.

For years, she dreamed to live by water, and when an opportunity in Jacksonville had a house on a lake, she jumped at the chance. Now it was a process of updating the house to her tastes. And that meant lots of DIY construction projects. Building a shower in a half-bathroom so my brother could have his own bathroom, painting kitchen cabinets because they were too old, and building a patio deck to have breakfasts by the lake. She loved seeing larks, swallows, and golden eagles snatch fish out of the water in the morning sun, when the water was glittering like diamonds.

The lake, its far shore curtained with evergreen trees, muted noises from the city. Engine roars, construction, honks, and foot traffic faded away, and in our backyard, the serenity seemed to leech stress right from your bones. You could stand still and hear silence, pure silence. Against that backdrop, I started inviting the neighbors over for dinner.

In a long farmhouse table, we ate and enjoyed the majesty of the trees and the lake. It was dinner with a view, and before long, we had neighbors, friends, and friends of friends asking when the next dinner was. They just popped up!

The sky was turning orange and purple by the time my mom's house, with its white brick facade, was coming into view. My neck, knees, and shoulders, stiff from being in the same position too long, cracked as I stretched out of the car.

She came out and hugged me tight, her jet-black hair smelling like the caramel-scented candles she put all over the house.

"How did it go?"

I hugged her back. It was good to be home.

"We have so much to talk about!" I smiled.

Work started early the next morning. She set a tiny cup of coffee on the counter, thick as syrup and black, with caramel-colored foam on top.

"I heard this joke recently," I said, taking a sip. "Oh, I missed this!"

"You didn't have it in Miami?" she asked without turning around, mixing purple onions into scrambled eggs.

"No time! It was go, go, go from the start. We had to set up the backyard tables the night before for the wedding, lugging thirteen tables into the backyard and the chairs to boot!"

"So what about this joke?" She scrambled eggs next to my coffee, where the purple of the onion mixed with the yellow of the yolk and turned the whole thing green.

"Oh yeah," I said, ignoring the eggs. "Cuban coffee is the reason crystal meth never took off in Miami!"

"It's the sugar. Not the caffeine. We always make it too sweet." She took out bread from the oven; the crust crackled as she tore off pieces of the loaf, handing me a piece. "How are the eggs?"

"Crunchy." I grimaced. "But the bread is delicious!"

The half-bath shared a wall with the garage, and since I was building a shower and needed access to the drains, the wall had to go. This had the unfortunate side effect that anyone who sat on that toilet would do it in front of the cars, tools, and Christmas decorations stored in the garage. After the drain for the new shower had been fixed, it was a relief to put drywall back up.

"Spapi's still coughing," said a text from Alicia. "His doctor referred him to a pulmonologist to see what's going on."

"That's good. They'll get to the bottom of it."

"I'm worried, babe. This isn't normal." Another text. "The other day, they went to Red Lobster and he bit into a piece of lobster that had a shell in it—he cracked his tooth! The weird thing is that he says he didn't feel any pain. He told the dentist, and he'll have to get it looked at."

"I'd be screaming!"

"Everybody would! This isn't normal."

On our dates, I got to appreciate just how difficult nursing school was through Alicia's eyes. You study ten hours a day, become familiar with an endless number of medication names and their chemistry within the body, and get exposed to every kind of patient at every age. It becomes an exercise in endurance. How much pressure can you handle? But it does make you grow. Doctors usually specialize, but the nursing program makes nurses ready for every specialty—

they go through it all. And having medical knowledge made her aware of serious possibilities in any symptom. To her, a cough was more than a cough; it could be a respiratory issue, a blockage in the lung or the windpipe, cancer, or an allergic reaction. She saw every possibility, and to her, a visit to any specialist was a cause for concern.

"He'll be okay, baby." I tried to sound reassuring. "You'll see that going to a pulmonologist, they'll find out the cause of whatever it is he has and he'll be over it in no time." I did not feel reassuring. "This is a good thing."

*Right?*

The messages stopped; she went back to class, and I went back to gluing CPVC pipes together.

For the rest of the week, we worked on the bathroom, closing walls and laying tile over them. Water and egg-shell-colored sand mixed together in a bucket, but I couldn't stop thinking about Robert's cough. As I smeared the grout mix over tiles, the thought of that persistent cough gnawed at me, like feeling the wind change before a rainstorm. Thoughts that make your hair stand on end.

"Hey! What do you know about grout?" I called him.

"More than you, that's for sure."

"Good! You can walk me through putting in on tile."

"Did you secure the tile first so it doesn't fall?"

"Err…yes?"

His laughter over the speaker bounced off the walls in the tiny bathroom. "Just use a sponge to apply and another one to wipe off the excess. You should be fine, if tiles don't start falling off the walls!"

"Thanks for that. How did it go at the pulmonologist?"

"Good. He doesn't know why the antibiotics and other medication didn't work. He's scheduled me to do a bronchoscopy."

"What's that?" I asked.

"That's where they stick a tube with a little camera down your throat and take a look into your lungs to see what's going on," he answered.

"Does it hurt?"

"They put you under. They say I won't feel a thing. Maybe some soreness in your throat when you come back up."

"What are they looking for?"

"They want to see what's going on in there. And if there's something, they'll take a sample and send it to the lab for analysis," he added. "Can you believe it, Mauricio? First, two weeks of bronchitis, then two weeks of pneumonia, and now this bronchoscopy thing. What the *heck*, man?"

At the end of that week, new shower, with river pebbles on the floor, stood in the corner of the bathroom. Shelves of freshly toasted wood flanked the shower, and my mom was tightening the last towel hook. "Lilies."

"Hmmm?"

"This bathroom should have lilies."

"Why lilies?"

"It speaks to me!" She smiled.

The next afternoon, the smell of caramelizing onions filled the kitchen. Next to that pan, an old pressure cooker sputtered steam, turning chicken bones into brown stock, building the layers of flavor that would be found in sauces, vegetables, and rice. On the fridge, a paper with menu items for the next dinner by the lake were crossed off as they were prepped and wrapped in plastic in the fridge.

"So tell me about her! How did it go at the dinner with her parents?" She sat across the counter from me, drinking her coffee.

"You would have loved being there! Her dad had a T-shirt that read, 'Ten Rules for Dating My Daughter.' As I was cutting oranges for the salad dressing, he went to the bathroom. Alicia got close to me, whispering, 'He wore that shirt on purpose. I tried to talk him out of it. I'm sorry!' So when he came back, he asked, 'You like my shirt?' and I don't know where it came from, Mom, but I saw, 'Rule 10: Anything you do to her, I'll do to you,' and I told him, 'I love it! I'm pretty open-minded.'"

"You didn't!" She snorted into her coffee, stifling a laugh.

"I swear I did! Either it worked or I would get kicked out of the house. But it paid off!" I said, shrugging.

"So you had to talk to him and get permission? You've never done that before, right?"

"No. First time. I know it's the old-fashioned way, and people don't do it much now, but it felt right, you know? There was a preacher online once that said something that stuck in my head: 'In life you always pay cost. Either you pay for it up front or life demands its payment from you after.'"

"It's true," she said, taking another sip of coffee. She sighed, her gaze lost in the mistakes of the men in her own past—the father that was never there to demand permission from boyfriends, and the husband who ran off with another woman, leaving her with two young boys. A twinge of pain shot across her face, gone as fast as it came, replaced with a smile and a singsong tone. "Mistakes cost. But enough about that. Tell me about her!"

Dark beer mixed into the chocolate cake batter in the bowl, turning the brown mix jet-black.

"She reminds me of you a little bit." I poured the batter on the cake pan. "She's had a difficult relationship with her father, and she's the type to give her whole heart to someone else, and she's been hurt by it before."

"Are you sure about her?"

"Do you like her?" I asked.

"It's not my place to sway you one way or another."

"Oh please, Mom! You've never been shy when I'm making a mistake with the wrong girl!"

"Answer the question, then!"

"Yes! Okay! I love her. I like her! You happy there?"

"Ay, mi niño!" She walked around the counter and hugged me. "Yes, I really like her for you. She stayed talking to me all night that Thanksgiving we spent with your friends."

"Really?" The oven, on preheat, beeped. "I don't remember that."

"I remember thinking, 'I would love one like this for Maury.' She was funny!"

I put the cake in the oven.

"Just be sure about her. I've been in a situation like that, and it hurts. You don't get over that easily."

"I know." I hugged her tight again. "I know. Now we got people coming tomorrow. Help me set the table?"

The next evening, a small crowd had gathered in the backyard. Neighbors and friends who knew about our secret little dinners brought newcomers to try the tasty menu by the lake at sunset. The cool evening breeze gained strength over the lake, and pines in the far shore swayed, dancing in that breeze. Bass jumped every few minutes, trying to catch a tasty fly for dinner, too fast for the newcomers to catch, darting below the waters, leaving only a ripple as evidence.

No one spoke much while watching the lake at sunset, choosing instead to be filled with the sound of rustling leaves, waves lapping against the shore, cicadas buzzing, or whatever else nature chose to present. Maybe they saw God's presence in those woods, or maybe nature's show spoke of Him, and that was enough.

Then came the food.

My mom and I brought out each course two plates at a time, running back and forth between the kitchen and the table. There were bowls of soup that changed color from white to pink, green mounds of arugula dotted with strawberry wedges, and knobs of goat cheese in olive oil. While they ate, we plated entrees in the kitchen—orange streaks of butternut squash puree surrounded a bed of spinach and kale, with strips of seared rib eye.

"Add the smoked salt flakes to the meat."

"It's not seasoned already?"

"Yeah, but the salt flakes add another texture, making the crust even crunchier. And the smoke goes well with the meat."

"You finish them. I'll pick up the plates."

We took the entrees once the empty plates were back in the kitchen. Guests waited impatiently to hear the reasoning behind the dish. We learned quickly that psychology, as much as cookery, played a part of the experience. If they knew a bit about the philosophy behind each dish, they could analyze it and it became more than just a plate of food; it became more meaningful, a memory they carried with them long after the flavor faded.

After entrees, I carried the Guinness cake to the table. The last course would have a show, served table-side. My mom set a tray next to the cake with sugar and blowtorch and vanilla ice cream. Cicadas rustled in the trees outside, starting the night. In the dining room, only a dim glow of bistro lights illuminated guests, and as the lights dimmed down, so did the conversation.

"The Guinness Company uses dark roasted barley in their beer. This is what lends the color and slight bitterness to the stout. We wanted to replicate that with this dessert."

I sprinkled sugar over the surface of the cake and, with the blowtorch, waved it back and forth, melting the sugar crystals, forming a crust.

"The cake already has dark beer, but it needs another texture component—crystallized sugar gives it that, like in a crème brûlée. And the heat from the torch gives a smokiness to the cake itself, making the roast barley in the beer come alive again."

I cut slices, and my mom served them with a dollop of ice cream.

"We serve this cake the way it's eaten at home, without pretension, just letting the flavors and textures do the talking. Please enjoy."

They ate and stayed talking for the next hour, reliving the meal and their favorite parts. After the last one left, asking when the next dinner would be, my mom got to washing dishes while I cleaned up the table.

There was a privilege in being able to do these events, to find an audience for the gifts God put in you. It was a pleasure to see others experience joy through our food. I grabbed the last crumpled napkin at the edge of the table, and my phone rang. It was Alicia, video-calling to see how it went.

"Hey, baby! We had a great night. Everybody loved the food!" I showed her the empty dining room.

"Babe."

When I looked at her face, her eyes were red, swollen from tears that still trickled down her cheeks. I grabbed the nearest chair.

"Spapi has lung cancer."

# Till We Hit Bottom

*Robert*

"You got a call from Barrios," she said, kissing me as I walked in the door.

"I was in meetings all day. First, the architect, he needs to get me new plans. Then his interior decorator wants to change one kind of white marble for another, and then a problem with the cabinet manufacturer! That job's been a complete mess, babe."

"Well, that's why you're there, honey," she said, dismissing everything I just said.

"Barrios's office wants you to go there tomorrow to go over the results of the bronchoscopy."

My throat tightened.

"You'll come with me?"

The pulmonologist's practice was in an old building from the sixties. The low ceilings and fluorescent light created dark corners everywhere, making the space feel tighter by the minute. Leila checked us in for the appointment, and I took a seat in the waiting room. Around us, waiting their turn were older folk clutching oxygen tank respirators and hacking wet, raspy coughs that drowned out *The View* on TV. Being in that place made my chest feel tight. For someone who worked outdoors, on top of roofs, feeling the beating sun and winds, I fought every instinct to run out. There was a stale smell of death in that place. Leila squeezed my hand, her reading glasses reflecting the light from her phone.

The door to the examination rooms opened, and a girl around Alicia's age, in navy scrubs and a sweater, came out holding a chart.

"Germroth? Robert?"

She didn't guide us into an examination room, but into his office. It was sparse and clean, with diplomas and awards hanging from the walls. "He'll be with you soon," she said, closing the door behind her.

Leila was again looking at her phone to pass the time, scrolling through Facebook and seeing photos of last week's assembly at her school—children in yellow and khaki uniforms smiling with macaroni sculptures and chairs made from sticks. After a few minutes of that, Dr. Barrios came in. He tried to work a smile on his face, but it never reached his eyes. After shaking our hands, he sat on his chair and took a deep breath. Something was wrong.

"So what kind of bronchitis is it? What do the tests show?"

"Robert," started out Barrios, "I'm afraid it's not bronchitis. The tissue sample we sent to the lab shows cancer. According to the results, you have non-small-cell lung cancer."

Everything after those words was muffled, like if someone was talking to you with your head underwater. I heard the news, and I heard the noise, but it never hit home. Leila squeezed my hand tight and bowled over in her chair; her phone clattered on the floor. She let out a long wail and gasped for air, as if an invisible hand had punched her in the stomach. And in that moment, all I could think was how beautiful she looked on our wedding, when we promised to be by each other through whatever came, "till death do us part."

"I won't be able to walk Alicia down the aisle," I said to myself. Now my eyes were stinging, tears starting to form in the corners.

"Wait, wait, wait!" yelled Dr. Barrios, throwing up his hands. "Stop! I haven't signed your death sentence, you know! Cancer research has come a long way. We're going to order a PET scan, and based on that, we have treatment options. Since it's located in the lung, we can cut it out."

"So we caught it early?" Leila asked, rummaging in her purse for tissues.

"The test will tell us more. But if you *just had* to have lung cancer, you want non-small cell. It's the better one, and it's slow-growing. We locate where it is—we know it's somewhere on the right lung—and cut it out. There are patients who have only one lung and still live just fine."

"Really?"

"The pope only has one lung."

"Huh! Look at that."

I looked over at Leila dabbing her eyes.

One question was still nagging me, and I was afraid to ask. "Doctor, my father died from brain cancer. Can you tell me with 100 percent certainty that this cancer is from smoking cigarettes and not genetic?"

"No. I can tell you 1,000 percent"—he emphasized *thousand*—"that this cancer is from smoking cigarettes."

That hurt. We were silent for some time.

"Okay, what's the next step? What do we do?" asked Leila.

"You'll be back here tomorrow for some breathing tests to determine your oxygen intake. That will help us with how to proceed with treatment. I'm going to send you to see a good friend of mine, Dr. Kaywin, who is one of the head oncologists at the new Miami Cancer Institute that just opened in January. But first, let's get that PET scan, because he's going to want to see it."

"What's a PET scan?"

"It's like an MRI that scans your whole body. Since cancer eats sugar like crazy, they will give you an IV or a drink with a radioactive contrast that mimics sugar. Cancer will go after that, and it will light up on the scan. That way, we'll be able to see where in the lung is the mass and how big," said Dr. Barrios. "We'll make an appointment after we get the results of the PET scan and go from there."

Leaving the doctor's office, Leila and I moved on autopilot, each in our little bubble, digesting the news. I don't remember getting in the car. I don't remember getting home.

"Who do we tell?" Leila asked. "My parents? Alicia and Robbie? What about Mauricio?"

"We're going to have to tell Alicia and Robbie."

*Cough cough.*

"She's in nursing school, and I'm going to need a nurse at home. Let's wait on telling the rest until we know more. Like Dr. Barrios said, we cut it out and get back to our lives."

"If only," she said dryly.

When Alicia got home from school that evening, before she could put her books in her room, Leila called her to the couch. From the dinner table I saw my wife sit her daughter down and tell her the news. Like her mother, she started crying.

"I had a feeling, you know?" she said, composing herself. "We read about it in school. When infections don't respond to antibiotics, then it's probably cancer."

And still, not one tear fell from Leila; it took everything she had not to cry in front of her daughter. She was like that when it came to Alicia. Throughout the divorce with her ex-husband and all the abuse he put them through, Leila always had to be the strong one for her kids. And she raised her daughter to be the same.

I love that woman.

The rest of the evening we spent answering Alicia's questions, trying to give her hope that we ourselves didn't really feel. The food we ordered for dinner went cold in the aluminum containers it came in; none of us ate that night.

A few days after the breathing tests at Barrios's, we had our appointment for the PET scan. The three of us went this time, feeling the impulse not to lose sight of one another.

Like Barrios's office, the hospital was built in the 1960s, with low ceilings, fluorescent lights, and too many patients. The outer walls were still painted with the original flamingo pink that was popular back then. Though the hospital boasted of 728 beds, it didn't count for walk-ins, the emergency department, and outpatient services on each floor. A constant buzz of doctors, nurses, family members, and trainees—some still in high school—shuffled on the marble hallways, trying not to bump into one another. Alicia led the way to radiology; since high school, she had been volunteering at the hospital and knew the layout better than most of the staff did.

We made it to a small waiting room with a sign on the door: DIAGNOSTIC IMAGING DEPARTMENT. After twenty minutes of waiting, a girl in green scrubs called us into another salon with beds separated by curtains. "You're on bed 8, Mr. Germroth!" said the young blond nurse. "Right around the corner. Follow me."

The nurse didn't look much older than Alicia.

"You're here for an PET scan, correct? With contrast."

"Yes." I took a seat on the bed. "Yes, with contrast."

"Perfect!" She closed the curtain so I could change into an exam gown. "One last question, handsome. What flavor would you like? We got orange, banana, coconut, and strawberry."

"Let me have the coconut. I love piña coladas."

She left as Leila and Alicia settled into their chairs.

"I can't wait to be done with this, babe." I grabbed Leila's hand, giving it a squeeze.

"Next time I get a piña colada will be in Ft. Myers next month. Can you picture it? You in your bikini, me sunbathing without half a lung."

Leila just squeezed my hand and smiled. I tried not to think about what got us here, before the bronchitis and the pneumonia. The more I shifted my focus to the PET scan, the more I pushed down the years of cigarettes and the fights Leila and I had to quit smoking. Every time I came home, she smelled cigarettes on my clothes, and I'd brush it off, saying it was the guys on the jobsite; they would smoke, and I'd be around them, telling them what to do. I told her that so often that I believed it myself. She never did.

It didn't help that as soon as Dr. Barrios said *cancer*, I remembered my dad. He died of brain cancer at fifty-seven, less than a year from my age now. At the end, he was too weak to move by himself—I had to carry him from his bed on the second floor of the house to the car to get his treatments. The room felt smaller.

"Where is that nurse with that drink?" I yelled. "Alicia, go see what's taking her so long."

"Be nice to Alicia. She's just as much in shock as the rest of us. The nurse will be here when she gets here. Calm down."

"I don't want to end up like my dad, babe."

"Try to think of something else."

"He died just a year older than I am now. I remember how hard he fought. He got us kids into church, kicked our butts to make something of ourselves, all the while he was going through chemo." My throat tightened. "How are we going to do this?"

Before Leila could answer, Alicia came back with the nurse.

"Okay, Mr. Germroth! I have your piña colada! Drink it and I'll be back in an hour. Once it's in your system, we can start the scan."

Before I could say anything, she was already out the door to tend to another patient. I stuck a straw in the Styrofoam cup and tasted a thick, chalky milkshake that was a mixture of coconut and concrete.

"How is it?" Leila asked.

"It's hard going down," I said. "I can't wait for Ft. Myers next month."

Once the drink was in my system, the technician guided me to the machine. A rectangular slab where I lay down was in front of a small circular tunnel. Laying my bare back on the metal table sent a shock up my spine. My teeth started chattering. One of the nurses, tightening her sweater over her scrubs, brought me blankets from a warming drawer. They strapped me down, and the machine slowly swallowed me, headfirst, into its tunnel.

It would be cozy enough to sleep if not for the loud whooshing noises of the magnets behind their casing moving at high hundreds of miles a minute. Even through the head-phones they gave me, it was loud!

"They'll find it, cut it out, and I'll get back to my life. Nothing to worry about."

And just like that, it was over.

"Okay, Mr. Germroth, we'll get you back to your room, and your doctor will schedule an appointment with you to go over the results!"

Back home, we continued our lives as if nothing happened in the surface. Leila went back to work, brought dinner in the evenings, and we ate. Fish soup on Wednesdays, rice and beans on Thursdays. Friday we went out; this week, it was the fish place by our house. It looked like a fish market in the Caribbean. As soon as you walked in, octopus, red snapper, diver scallops, and swordfish steaks were on ice in a glass case. Nautical flags covered every inch of the ceiling, and next to the door, a life-size wooden pirate statue flashed his missing teeth to greet you. We saw to the back, away from the main crowd, where we could talk.

"I'll have the teriyaki salmon," said Leila, her head buried in the menu.

"Okay."

We had settled into a quiet unease since coming home from the scan, like a sour pit in your stomach that wouldn't go away.

"Stop playing with your hair," Leila said. "You'll go bald!"

I slammed my knuckles on the table, making the silverware jump, and some water.

"Sorry."

She said nothing, wiping the spilled water with our napkins instead.

"Any word from the doctor?"

"No," she said coolly, engrossed in the fish croquettes on the menu.

"I'm sure it'll be all right. Right?"

"Leila."

"Can you ask for more napkins, please?"

During the day, I focused on the jobs. I convinced myself that there was nothing else I could do but wait, so I might as well focus on what was at hand, and right now, that was to get three houses renovated for my clients. One of them had an issue with a water pump in a bathroom; I would have to send my plumber. Another house had issues with the electrical. The electrician hadn't shown up again today and wouldn't answer my calls. So I could scream my frustrations at his voice mail.

But at night, when the coughing was worse and I sat up in bed, there was no one to scream at. And the fear of what the results would bring made my hair stand on end. At the same time, my mother in South Carolina was getting a heart valve replacement. Her heart was weakening, and her doctor scheduled the operation for the next day. Between my visits to the jobs, I would call my sister Joan and get updates on her condition.

"IT KILLS ME I CAN'T GET UP THERE, JOAN!" I screamed at the phone. "QUIET DOWN FOR A SECOND—I'M ON THE PHONE!" A chipping hammer behind me drowned out my voice.

"Oh, hush, Bobby! You got enough on your plate. Between me and Howie and Joyce, we're taking care of Mama. We'll tell you what's going on with her. You just take care of yourself. Leila sent me a picture of you in the hospital—you're looking skinny!"

Leila had told them that I was going through a health issue, but we agreed not to say anything else to anyone until we knew just what we were dealing with. After we told Alicia and Robbie, cancer became much more real in our lives, like a stranger in our home that just wouldn't leave. Whenever they saw me, they would fake a smile and rarely looked me in the eyes. I didn't want that.

41

By the evening, Leila walked through the door with cantina.

"I'm hungry!" She smiled, setting the plastic bag filled with aluminum tins on the counter, sending the smell of fried fish deep into my nostrils. Leila set plates while I greedily lifted the paper lids and waited for her to sit.

"How was your day, babe?" I asked.

"Rice, now!" She held out her plate. "Pretty please?" Batting her eyelashes.

As I loaded up her plate, the kitchen phone rang. Leila set down her plate half-filled and answered.

"Hello?"

"Yes."

"Uhuh?"

I waved to her to see who it was, and she waved my hand away.

"Okay. Tuesday, then, 3:00 p.m.? Thank you."

She sat back down.

"That was Barrios's office. The results are ready."

*****

I looked at my feet, sitting in Barrios's waiting room. There was no one else waiting with me today. Only me and *The View* on TV. Leila would be coming anytime. I pushed her to get out of work early so we could hear the results together. But until she got there, it was Joy Behar and me.

"It's one thing to talk to Jesus, it's another thing when Jesus talks to you," she said over the TV.

"I need some of that right now," I said to myself. The gnawing fear of what the tests would show was making my leg restless. I looked at the door. No Leila.

"Hey, you on your way?"

"Stuck in traffic!"

"Well, hurry up! We're going to hear good news today!" I forced myself to smile.

"Mr. Germroth, we're ready for you!" said Dr. Barrios's assistant, standing in the doorway to his office.

"Can we wait a few minutes? My wife is still on her way."

"She can meet you in Dr. Barrios's office. I'll take her there when she arrives."

I got up to follow her.

"You heard the lady. Get over here."

I sat in his office, same chair as last time.

"Dr. Barrios will be with you in a few minutes."

I rolled my wedding ring over my finger to pass the time, just to give my hands something to do. I imagined life after the operation. Would I breathe differently with one lung? I used to play with the kids when they were little, chasing them in the park. Would I be able to do that with my grandkids when they came? How about the jobs? Would I be able to get back on a roof again? Much less get down?

"Robert, honey." Leila was tapping me on the shoulder. "You okay?"

"Now that you're both here, he'll be with you in a moment," said the assistant, halfway out the room already. "He wanted to speak with you both."

Before anyone else came in, Leila grabbed my hand and looked into my eyes. "We're going to be okay."

I smiled.

Dr. Barrios opened the door, followed by Dr. Juvenal. "Hey, guys," said Barrios, grabbing a chair behind his desk. Juvenal took the chair next to him. "We got the test results back from the PET scan. Let me show you." He held the negative to a light box and turned it on. A familiar torso, lungs, and other organs were shown by the silver edges of their shapes. Within the organs, white spots dotted almost everywhere.

Barrios took a deep breath.

"There's no good way of saying this. You see these dots?"

We nodded.

"This is cancer lit up by the contrast. The last time we talked, we suspected it was in the lungs. This scan shows a completely different picture. That's why I asked Juvenal to join us."

"How bad is it?" Leila asked, squeezing my hands tight.

"When you see the spots light up like this in several different organs, it means it's traveled," said Juvenal, pointing to the smaller masses in the hip and spine. "It's stage 4."

"Stage 4?" we both yelled, wide-eyed in disbelief. "But we caught it early!" "There were no symptoms!" "I felt fine!"

"Sometimes it's asymptomatic," said Barrios, drooping his shoulders. "In other cases, the pneumonia and bronchitis could have been a symptom."

"So what does that mean?"

"It means we can't cut it out," said Barrios. "It's already traveled from your right lung to your brain, hip, spine, jaw, and these other small markers."

"But wait a minute!" I slammed my hand on the armrest. "Can't we cut out the large mass and treat the smaller areas with chemotherapy?"

"You'd never survive it," answered Juvenal just as quick. Finality in his voice. "An operation like that will weaken you considerably. And the recovery is monthslong. It would leave you too weak for chemo, and in that time, the cancer still spreads."

"So much for the piña colada in Ft. Myers," I muttered in defeat.

Leila and I stayed silent, taking in the information. It still felt surreal. The hairs on our arms stood on end.

"So what do we do?" asked Leila, dabbing her eyes with a tissue.

"I'm putting you in contact with Dr. Kaywin at Miami Cancer Institute. He's the head oncologist and a good old friend of mine from medical school. He's the best person to handle your treatment, and he will tell you guys the game plan," answered Barrios, leaning forward in his chair.

"Okay, then!" chimed Leila, taking charge. "There's a plan. We can do this!"

"One thing you have to both remember: you're in for the fight of your lives," said Juvenal, grabbing Leila and me by the hand. "Through this process, you have to remember that we're here for you. Day or night. Call us!"

After a few minutes and a few more tears from Leila and me, we left their office and headed home. We drove home in silence, wide-eyed and taking deep breaths, listening to the sound of raindrops falling on the roof of the car and the constant hum of the engine.

"When the doctor says you have cancer, all you hear is, 'You're going to die unless this thing you have goes away.'"

"Please don't talk like that, Robert."

"Isn't it true?"

The rain drowned out every other noise.

Over the next few days, all we could think of was meeting Dr. Kaywin. And once we met him, everything would make more sense. Leila went to work, focusing on her students and staff meetings. I started getting shooting pains in my chest and staying home; my guys would supervise the jobs for me. Finally, the phone rang from Miami Cancer Institute, our appointment for the day after tomorrow having been confirmed.

Leila drove, pulling into a covered driveway with valet parking. An attendant in khaki shirt and black pants opened Leila's door and helped her out. As we walked into the lobby, it was easy to get lost in the view. There were forty feet of glass windows flooding the space with natural light. It looked more like a five-star hotel than it did a cancer wing at a hospital. There were couches and coffee tables in open areas right in front of each department, and a complimentary coffee bar as people waited for their appointments.

A volunteer, dressed in lime-green polo and beige khakis, led us to Dr. Kaywin's office. It became a habit now to sit alone for a few minutes, waiting for the doctor. Finally, the door opened and a man with oxblood leather loafers and slacks walked in. The hair on his head was mostly gone from old age, but behind his glasses, piercing gray eyes looked back at us.

"You must be Robert." He smiled kindly, and without pity. It gave me the impression that he saw me, and not the cancer, when he was talking to me. It was refreshing.

He sat Leila and me down while he and his assistant, Shannon, pored over our records.

"Okay, Robert, so you have non-small-cell lung cancer," started out Dr. Kaywin, clapping his hands. "You have a really tough fight ahead."

"Dr. Kaywin," I interrupted. "How bad is it, really? We don't know what to expect here."

"There is no cure. It's stage 4 and spread to your jaw, hipbone, adrenal gland, and also your brain. There's a section in your chest that's compressing a major blood vessel—that's why you're having chest pains."

I took a deep breath, preparing myself.

"Let me put it this way: You are like a man on the edge of a cliff, hanging on by his fingernails. We have a lot of work ahead of us just to get you off the edge. From now on, you have to cut out any negativity, any stress, right out of your life."

"How long do I have left? I…"

He held up his hand to stop me. "I don't like giving my patients a timeline. It gets in their heads and complicates things."

"Please," I pleaded. "If you had to say?"

Kaywin paused.

"There is no cure, but let's hope you're here next January."

"It's April now…eight months? So what do we do? What's the treatment plan?" I asked.

We were in yet *another* doctor's office, trying to get a grip on how bad the situation was, and every time we found out that it was worse than we thought.

"Mr. Germroth, my first advice to you is to get your last will and testament, medical power of attorney, and financial power of attorney done. You need to get your affairs in order first. *Then* we can talk about treatment."

If you've ever built sandcastles in the beach, you know that eventually a wave comes and washes it all down. This doctor was the third wave. Leila and I had nothing else to hold on to. She looked at the floor while holding my arm.

Dr. Kaywin grabbed our hands, pulled Shannon closer, and made us huddle together. "One thing you must remember," he said, looking at us straight in the eyes. "We are a team. And we are going to fight this thing together!"

I don't remember how we got home. My mind kept replaying his words: *There is no cure.* And then it hit me; before anything else, he wanted me to have my affairs in order because the possibility of me dying was almost certain! This was it, the death sentence.

I dragged my feet to the hall bathroom. I needed a moment alone, and I didn't want Leila to see me. Everything had finally built up, and I couldn't take any more bad news. In the bathroom, I stood in front of the sink and stared at the face in the mirror. My body started shaking, as I felt every word from the doctors talking about my life, and how it was being taken away from me moment by moment. My face contorted, flushed, and I huddled over the sink, weeping. I remember every time I lied to my wife about the cigarettes, ashamed now what I allowed to come over my family. The whimpers echoed off the tiles, and the guilt of bringing this on my wife tore at me. I felt responsible for every tear she shed. Whatever the future held because of this, I knew I was responsible for their pain.

And in my tears, I cried out to God. The Bible says that He "is not far from any one of us," and I needed Him now. There was nothing left but to weep and cry out to Him. I heard a small voice in my spirit saying, "Repent."

In that moment, I begged forgiveness for everything, for the lies, for the cigarettes, for allowing so many things to come between Him and me. With all that I am, I begged for His forgiveness.

"Father, You gave King Hezekiah fifteen years when he was on his deathbed. I want fifteen years."

There was silence.

"If I'm not getting that, then heal me. Right now. I know You can do it."

Silence.

"Okay, then, until I hear from You, I'm going to follow the doctor's instructions, until You tell me something different."

Finally, I had peace.

# The Fight of Your Life

*Leila*
*Twenty-Two Years Ago*

"Yeah, Mom, he's a really nice guy! We went out to this little seafood restaurant, and he was great. Getting to a date has been…it's been tough! We were planning this for weeks, and finally we could line up babysitters for the same night."

I scrubbed the last bowl off the sink, the smell of lemon filling the air. I dried my hands and grabbed the phone pinned between my shoulder and ear.

"He even has a cute butt!" I smiled, keeping an ear on the kids playing in the den. "There's just one problem: he smokes."

"Uh-oh!" came my mother's voice. "I know that's a big deal for you."

"Yeah, I know!" I said, pacing around my kitchen, letting the cord wrap around my shoulders. "Funny thing, though, I asked him, 'So what would it take for you to quit?' And you know what he told me?"

"What?"

"'All you gotta do is ask.' So I told him, 'Okay, I'm asking.' Can you believe it?"

He was so handsome then. The man who would become my husband, who was already a father to his blond blue-eyed boy. His auburn hair and piercing blue eyes glinting against his suntanned skin. Even before we met, his skin was tanned; as a kid, he grew up surfing in James Island, up in South Carolina, and now he was tanned from construction sites, going up and down roofs all day. Yelling at his workers, then rolling up his sleeves and working right along with them. A dead ringer for Patrick Swayze, without the dance skills.

He kept his promise about smoking, until he didn't.

## *Eight Years Ago*

Eight years into our marriage, he started a new job. Much more money, but much more stress. He would leave the house at six in the morning and wouldn't get back until after sunset. My South Carolina husband, who did not speak a word of Spanish, was supervising multiple construction crews who barely spoke broken English. They would speak to one another in Spanish, and he couldn't follow, feeling isolated while surrounded by his coworkers. Gradually he would come, and the sweet, sticky smell of tobacco hung all over his clothes. Over the years, his truck became forbidden to the rest of the family, and every Saturday, during our day to do yard work at the house, he would have to go to Home Depot for something. It was always something.

One Saturday in particular, I was looking for him all over the house, in our office, the kitchen, and the backyard. He was nowhere. I went behind the shed, where he kept the ladders, wheelbarrows, and shovels, thinking he was organizing his tools, and I saw the blue-and-white-checkered pattern of his shirt around the corner. As I followed it, there he was, a lit cigarette in his hand.

"Nice!" I felt my face warm. "So it wasn't just the guys at work smoking around you, or your boss smoking in your car while you were driving him around. You promised me!"

"Leila...," he started, tossing the cigarette on the ground and stomping on it.

"No! Leila nothing! You know how I feel about cigarettes!"

He wrapped one leg behind the other.

"You know that they cause cancer. I already had one marriage end because someone betrayed their word. I won't have it a second time!" I headed for the house.

"Leila!" He darted behind me, cutting me off at the door.

"Move!" I screamed. "Don't you know how this makes me feel? Do you think I want to see you sick or with a hole in your throat or dead?"

"LEILA!" he said, trying to get a word in.

"Real nice! Robert!" I went around him and into the house. Out of the corner of my eye, I saw him crush the packet of cigarettes and throw it into the neighbor's yard. I closed the door.

## *Now*

After dinner, I washed the same bowls, and the same lemon fragrance filled the kitchen.

"Leila?"

I turned around, and Robert was standing behind me, his eyes red and his face flushed, having just come out of the bathroom. I knew my husband well enough to know he'd been crying. I didn't need to see his red eyes and puffy cheeks

51

to know. He walked past me and grabbed a glass from the dish rack, filling it with water. As he drank, his clothes hung loose around his shoulders.

"Leila…" He took a seat at the counter. "We have to get a grasp on this thing. We need to get into a spirit-filled church, one that believes in healing. We can't do this without God."

"Okay," I said. "We always talked about finding a church. Where do you want to go?"

"I don't know." He took a deep breath and let out a small cough. "When does Mauricio get back? We need to ask him where he goes."

"I think Alicia mentioned that he'll get back in a few days. She says he's looking for a place to stay with his friends."

"We have an extra bedroom here. Would you be okay if he stayed here?"

"You can't be serious, Robert. We've known him a few weeks at the most!"

He held out his hand, and when I grabbed it, he pulled me onto the chair next to him. I felt the familiar calluses from years of construction work; now they also felt thinner, with skin giving way to the bone beneath.

"I'm serious!"

That was completely out of character for my husband. With Alicia's ex-boyfriends, he always told them, "I'm not afraid to go to jail, and I'm not afraid to go to hell for my family." This was the man who grabbed her ex-boyfriend by the arm, walked him to the archway of Alicia's room, and pointed to the grout line and said, "Your world ends at this line. You do not cross this line." Now he was talking about offering the new boyfriend the room right next to hers.

"Why?"

He didn't say anything, just stared at me.

"They've only been dating six weeks, Robert. Are you sure about this?"

"He constantly drives back and forth between here and Jacksonville every two weeks to be with Alicia. And when he's here, he's sleeping on friends' couches." Our fingers entwined, his thumb caressing mine. "I would feel better with another man in the house. And though I could not, for the life of me, tell you why, I feel a peace with this kid."

"Okay, honey, if you're sure about this, I'll tell him when he gets back."

Robert nodded and rested his head on my shoulder. "We need to get into a spirit-filled church."

"I know, honey. We will," I said, caressing the back of his hand.

He went to the couch and took a nap. Every day he had less energy to do things, and his breath got quick, wheezing, like his body couldn't get enough of it. Dr. Barrios explained that with the cancer, getting oxygen would be an issue; it was common in patients for their lungs to fill with fluid and have a lot of difficulty breathing. It broke my heart to see him like that.

I went to my office and sat at my desk, arranging papers for the end of the school year and focusing on Alicia's graduation from nursing school. At the beginning of June, my kids would leave for the summer, and before then there would be the end-of-year assembly, banquets, final exams, and graduation. Alicia would also have her pinning ceremony and graduation, so I'd need to make a plan with my parents to go support her. There was plenty to keep my mind busy. Busy was good. Busy meant that I could escape, at least for a little while, the new reality of my husband choking to death on our couch. Busy was very good. I kept going through the plans in my head when the oncologist met with us. We had a plan! He'd get chemo. He'd be back to normal. All I had to do was stay busy on the plan. As long as I was busy, I was not thinking of him dying, or having to bury him, and with him the life we built together. Summers in Ft. Myers, Christmases, the trips to South Carolina to see his family, our gardening Saturdays. The papers became blurry as tears ran down my cheeks. The thought of burying him, and with him our future, made my hands shake. Him walking Alicia down the aisle one day, waking up each morning to his warmth by my side, feeling loved by him. All that gone.

Busy was good.

Being a teacher for over twenty-five years, I had a great ability for organization. In my classes I set calendars for school events, student assignments, professional development commitments, and I did it well. Things were neatly in their corresponding, color-coded binder, and every important paper filed away for easy retrieval. So with this situation, I did what came natural: I got a binder. Once Robert entered the system at the Miami Cancer Institute, their support staff called us every day to confirm appointments, so I made a calendar of his appointments for the month. Every piece of paper they would give us, I would find a place for it. I made it my mission to follow the plan and track every appointment, medication, then take notes on his diet and sleeping patterns, whatever was needed to make sure that any information that doctors would need to take care of my husband, I had it on hand.

That evening, the phone rang from the hospital, confirming an appointment for a jaw biopsy for the mass in his jaw. An MRI and CT scans to get more information on where the cancer was in his body. It became clear that there were going to be entire days spent in the hospital before we were going to get treatment of any kind, just tests. It seemed like an onslaught of medical assistants and coordinators that called the house wanted to schedule him for another test, and then another. Meanwhile, the cancer was still growing. I would jot the appointments in the binder. Then they would reschedule, another note in the binder.

Meanwhile, he was getting sicker.

For the rest of that week, Robert barely slept. He would keep tossing and turning in bed, wheezing and going to the bathroom, waking me up each time he did. I could hear him coughing and clearing his throat every few minutes, and he kept complaining of something being caught in his throat.

When I came home from work, he would be sitting in his recliner, with a lost look on his face, or at the kitchen table, hunched over. Seeing him like that, looking defeated, made me angry. On top of not sleeping already, I saw him shrivel down before my eyes. My husband, who cracked the whip at work and kept us on our toes at home. I was losing him.

"Sit up straight! How are you going to get better hunching over like that?" But he brushed me off and cleared his throat. I was losing my husband, and he was doing nothing to get back to us. Back in our office, I printed the schedule and his list of medicines. If he wasn't going to put effort into getting better, I would put double the work. The plan was going to work. Get him his medicines, get him through his appointments, and on to chemo. Then I'd get my husband back.

*Just stick to the plan.*

"Mrs. Germroth?" I heard a knock on my classroom. Mrs. Lee, the young language arts teacher for the fourth graders, stood in the doorway.

"I'm not your teacher anymore, Esther." I smiled

"Sorry, force of habit!" She kept her head bowed, forcing a smile. "I heard about your husband. I'm so sorry!" She walked into my classroom. The kids were already dismissed, and she was leaving for the day. On one shoulder she carried an overstuffed tote bag with assignments and lesson plans for the next day. In her other hand she carried a small green gift bag with the ruffled paper covering the gift inside.

"I know you're going through a very difficult time. A few years ago, my sister went through cancer and somebody at our church gave us this book," she said, laying the gift bag on my desk.

"Esther, thank you so much!" My jaw dropped. "I had no idea about your sister. You didn't say anything."

"It's always hard to talk about, especially when you're going through it." She folded her arms together, hugging the tote bag tighter. "Please, it's okay. The important thing is that you pay attention to this book. I don't know if you've ever heard of Joel Osteen. He's this big pastor out in Texas."

"Sure! My husband and I went to see him a few years ago at the American Airlines Arena when he was giving a conference here."

"Oh, good!" Her eyes lit up, and her arms relaxed. "Well, this is the story of how his mom was diagnosed with cancer. The doctors told the family that there was nothing more they could do for her. To take her home and spend as much time with her as possible before she died."

"Okay."

"But here's the important thing: she didn't die! She started believing in what the Bible says about healing and, in the face of impossible odds, that God is greater than any diagnosis. She's been alive for more than twenty years since that diagnosis!"

"Oh my goodness!" I got up from my chair and hugged her. "Thank you! I'll read it and share it with Robert. He's going through a lot right now."

"You both are, Leila. This isn't easy on anyone." She caressed my arm. "Anyways, I just wanted to share with you and let you know that all of us are pulling for you and your family. Speaking of, why aren't you with them now? It's after dismissal. Go home!"

I sat back down in my chair, reorganizing the quizzes I was grading before she came it. "Not just yet." I smiled. Just…not yet. A few more minutes. Thanks again for the book, Esther." I hugged her again before she left.

It hadn't hit me until now. Work was the only part of my life that was normal anymore. The only part that was structured and where cancer hadn't broken in. And right now, my classroom felt like the safest place in the world.

"Hang in there!" came her reply, and she left down the hallway. "And read the book!" could be heard from down the hall.

That evening, I picked up cantina from the corner market—mashed potatoes, braised chicken, and a chicken soup for Robert. As I was setting up the table, Alicia came out of her room and started unpacking the food from its Styrofoam containers.

"How was he today?" I asked.

"You really want to know?" she said dryly. "He slept most of the morning. Barely spoke a word to me, and as I was trying to study, all I heard was him screaming at somebody on the jobsite over the phone. Whoever Eddie is, I feel sorry for him."

"Eddie is his supervisor. When Robert is away from a jobsite, he leaves Eddie in charge to oversee things," I said. "Robert! Dinner is ready!"

Robert got up from his recliner, his black DADD (Dads Against Daughters Dating) shirt hanging loose on his body. Dressed in jean shorts and white socks, he looked small for his clothes, like a child wearing his brother's hand-me-downs. Normally, he weighed a hundred and ninety. At his last weigh-in, he barely reached a hundred and forty. He slowly shuffled his feet to the table, taking his usual seat while I made his plate.

"How was your good day, babe?"

"Good!" he growled, knowing anything else would get him in trouble.

I gave him a small kiss on the lips, gingerly, because the mass in his chin had grown and pushed his lips higher on his face.

"Did that hurt?"

"No, but everything feels weird in my mouth, like it's out of place."

He put mashed potatoes on the tip of his fork and carefully, slowly nibbled bits of food at a time.

On good days, what normally took thirty minutes to eat became an hour and a half. A few times he would ask me to microwave his plate because the food got cold while he ate.

"I'm not hungry, babe."

Today was not a good day.

He pushed his plate forward, rested his head in his hands, and closed his eyes.

"Mom, remember that my pinning ceremony is this Friday and graduation is on Saturday. Can we go to Flashback Diner after graduation?"

"Robert." I nudged his thigh.

"Hmmm?"

"Can you be a part of the conversation?"

"What did you say?" came his sluggish reply.

"We'll see how your dad feels, Alicia," I said, stabbing a chicken thigh with my fork a little too hard.

"Spapi." Alicia turned to him. "Can we please go? I love that place, and it's my graduation."

"We'll see if I have the energy," Robert said, his head still in his hands.

"Robert, sit up straight!" I yelled. "And get your head out of your hands, please! We're having dinner!"

Begrudgingly, Robert sat up a little more and started picking at his food but eating none of it.

"Alicia, your dad is having a lot of trouble breathing, and he gets tired really easily. We'll see how he does the day of your graduation, honey."

"When is Mauricio getting here?" Robert interrupted.

"Tonight!" Alicia chimed in faster. "He's already by, driving down!"

"He's coming straight here, right?" Robert coughed between sips of his tea.

I don't know who was more excited to see him, my daughter, who finally did her hair and put on some makeup, or my husband, who kept darting his eyes to the front window, looking for a red car.

When he pulled into our driveway, we saw Alicia sprinting in flip-flops, jumping into his arms, squealing with glee.

"You think she missed him?" I nudged Robert with an elbow.

"Not nary a bit." His bony elbow digging into my ribs, smiling. It was the first smile I'd seen on his face all week.

"Well?" Robert was tugging at my arm. "Let's go say hi!"

"Would you give them a minute? You remember what it's like at their age."

"Oh, right. Hormones."

After a few minutes, we joined them on the porch. Mauricio spoke of his trip, his family up in Jacksonville, and how things were here. Then he and Robert got into talking about the home-improvement projects, with Mauricio explaining how he made an opening in a wall or added a faucet, which made Robert laugh and call him a clumsy mess. Alicia would get all offended and defend Mauricio, which would make Robert laugh more, and for a second, my husband forgot he had cancer.

"Stay with us. For as long as you like!" I found myself blurting out in the middle of their conversation.

"Wait. What?" came his reply, still holding Alicia's hand.

"We know you're staying with friends for a few days, on their couch. But we have a spare bedroom no one is using. That way, you don't have to pack up and go to a different house every two days."

Mauricio looked at Alicia, looking for reassurance in her eyes, then at Robert. "Leila, are you sure? I don't want to be an imposition."

I looked at the smile on my husband's face. My daughter, who had her arms shamelessly wrapped around his. I met his eyes, which shone hazel in the sunset.

"Positive!"

A few days later, we drove to Alicia's pinning ceremony. Nova Southeastern University had banners guiding the parents to park in the garage closest to the auditorium.

"Spapi, we're going to be late! Hurry up! The ceremony is in twenty minutes!" yelled Alicia, the *click click click* in her heels echoing off the concrete ceiling and floors. "Mami, I need you to help me with the coat and the dress!"

The faster she walked toward the building, the farther behind we left Robert.

"Leila!" Robert panted. "STOP! I need to catch my breath." He stood still for a few minutes, trying to breathe, clutching his chest and wincing. Last night, after Alicia and Mauricio went to their rooms, Robert complained of chest pains every time he lay down. "It's like knives stabbing my chest," he said, massaging his sternum.

Alicia was pacing, tapping her shoes on the sidewalk, trying to hurry her dad but not wanting to make him worse. She made eyes at me, pleading to hurry him up.

"Leila, you guys go ahead and get her ready. I'll stay with Robert," said Mauricio. He took Robert's arm and walked alongside him, slowly.

In the lobby, hundreds of girls in white coats were greeting one another, taking photos with their families, and shrieking in excitement that they had finished their program. I helped Alicia with her coat and looked her over, making sure she didn't miss any details, the way I did when she was in kindergarten.

"Did you put on lipstick?"

"Err, no. I forgot."

"Do me a favor and go to the bathroom!" I said, pulling lipstick from my purse and shoving it in her hands. "You are not going to have graduation pictures looking like a corpse!" Like me, she had very fair alabaster skin, and with her long straight chestnut hair, her skin looked even whiter.

As she darted into a bathroom, Mauricio and Robert walked slowly into the lobby.

It was the first public function since his diagnosis. Robert looked uncomfortable in his suit, which was two sizes too big for him, and his face filled with wrinkles from weight loss and lack of sleep. Mauricio, with one hand on Robert's back, brought him to me. Robert, looking around for Alicia, stood next to me.

"Bathroom?"

"Lipstick." I rolled my eyes.

"Ah, every time." He took a deep breath. "I need to sit down," he told Mauricio, who took him to a bench nearby to wait for the start of the ceremony. Alicia came back, hand in hand with Valerie, and her family. Valerie, Alicia's best friend in nursing school, spent the last two years at my kitchen table in a study group. She and Alicia took the program together and kept each other motivated through the hardest parts. She already knew about Robert's condition, but no one except us had seen him since the diagnosis.

"Hey, Leila!" she said, hugging me. "Hi, Robert!" Not sure whether to kiss his cheek or even touch him. Finally, she leaned to a light, awkward hug.

"Hello," Robert said gruffly, trying to pass a smile. Before they could say any more, Valerie's family huddled around us, gabbing about the ceremony and where the graduates were going to sit. Taking a chance, Valerie pulled me aside.

"Oh my god, Leila! Alicia told me, but I had no idea he would look this bad!"

"It's been really tough," I replied, stealing looks at him over my shoulder.

"He looks a hundred years old! Has he been sleeping? And why does he have a cane?"

"No. No sleep. A few days ago, we were in the kitchen and he was listening to some old country song from when he was a kid. He tried to pull a dance move and we heard a loud crack! The next day we went to see the doctor and he ended up having a fracture in his hip. So my dad had an old cane in his house and gave it to him."

"Oh my god!" said Valerie, her hands over her mouth. "So on top of the cancer, he broke his hip?" She stole glances at his chin and the golf-ball-size tumor growing out of it.

"It's because of the cancer, said the doctor. It got into his hip and weakened it. The same thing happened with his jaw. When we went to see the periodontist, he told him, 'Your jaw is so brittle. Don't get in a car accident, and don't get in a fight with anyone, or you'll lose it.'"

"Oh, wow!" Her eyes wide.

No matter how much love or concern people who knew us showed, it was hard to talk about his cancer. With every new person that approached to hear me whisper the story and express their sympathies, I could feel the cancer growing in our lives. And the more I talked about where the cancer was spread all over his body, the farther and farther my husband felt.

"It's starting!" said Alicia, locking arms with Valerie, pulling her away. "We have to go sit down. We'll see you guys later!"

We hugged the girls goodbye and joined the hundreds of other family members looking for seats. Finally, the president of the university spoke about the rigors of the bachelor's degree in nursing and how a recent study called it the most difficult bachelor's program in the nation, harder even than mechanical engineering. I could already picture Alicia's justified smugness at hearing those words; every day she complained at how hard nursing school was. Robert took quick shallow breaths. He squeezed my hand tight, letting me know how much pain he was in. But here we were—we made it to her graduation! And at least he was a part of it.

After the ceremony, we took pictures in front of the shark statue that faced the auditorium.

"So can we go to Flashback Diner to celebrate?" she asked expectantly. "After all, I did graduate from the *hardest* bachelor's program!"

"Honey, we would," I sighed, shrugging, "but your dad is in a lot of pain and can't breathe. He needs to go home."

"Oh," she said, looking at the floor. "Okay."

I knew how much she wanted to celebrate with us, like we'd done with every major accomplishment in her life. If Robert had not been sick, we would have already been at the restaurant, Robert with a glass of wine in his hand and ordering champagne to celebrate his little girl. Instead, we got to take her home and promise to celebrate her success sometime in the future.

"Babe, it's okay," Mauricio chimed in. "I'll go pick up Thai food, and we can celebrate in. I know it's not the ideal, but we'll make the best of it."

She nodded.

Back at home, over pad thai and coconut chicken soup, Alicia was picking at her plate, still with the diner on her mind. Robert spooned broth as best as he could with the tumor in his jaw; he had no appetite and barely spoke. Finally, he slammed his hand on the table.

"Congrats, Coosie, you're a nurse!" he said. "I'm so proud of you!" he added, holding back tears.

Alicia stood up and hugged him tight. "You're the only graduation present I need."

His lower lip started quivering. Squeezing her waist as hard as he could.

"Mauricio!" he asked, wiping his eyes. "What's the name of the church we're going to tomorrow?"

"Al-ha n' Om-eha shur-sh!" he answered from his plate of mushroom and noodles.

"Give him a second, Spapi! He ordered something called the Spicy Phoenix! Look at his eyes—he's crying!"

Robert started laughing, really laughing, a deep, throaty laugh that made him slap his thighs. "You're a mess, man!" he said, wiping tears from his eyes.

"Leave him alone, Spapi! Don't pick on him!"

As everyone laughed, Mauricio was wiping sniffles from his nose and tears from his eyes.

"That can't taste good!" I turned to the poor kid, refilling his glass of water.

"Alpha and Omega Church!" he said after gulping the entire glass. "And it's delicious! Thank you, Leila." He grabbed the water and gulped it down. "It gets spicier with every bite. I ordered it with the same level of heat Thai people eat."

"Why?" I asked, refilling his water again.

"It's an *experience*!" He laughed.

"I'll bet it is!" said Alicia. "You're going to give yourself an ulcer."

"He'll be sorry in an hour, Coosie. Just you wait. For the church, at what time do we need to be there? Does it last long?"

"It starts at ten thirty, usually for an hour. Why?"

"No reason," he said, taking a deep breath and massaging his chest.

Robert didn't sleep that night either. I felt him every thirty minutes get up from bed, go to the recliner, try to sleep there, and come back to bed to find another comfortable position. Every night he was trying to find a comfortable position. Between the pain in his hip, where cancer was digging into his bones, and the pain in his chest, from cancer compressing his organs, he was desperate.

Every night I kept going over the plan in my head. "He has the port surgery this week," I told myself. "That's one step less, then he can get chemo and we can get closer to normal."

He left for the recliner again.

It was finally morning. He shaved and showered, wanting to look his best.

"Leila, what if I can't breathe?" he said, buttoning his dress shirt.

"Don't think about that now. We're going to be late." I clipped on my earrings.

"It's a big church. What if the air conditioner goes out?" Tightening his belt to a new hole to keep his pants from falling.

"Then I'll take you out to the car and turn on the air, Robert! Now, would you please get a move on? We're going to be late!"

By 9:45 a.m., Mauricio and Alicia were already dressed and waiting on us in the kitchen. I turned on the car and blasted the AC to the coldest setting so Robert could breathe. Alicia met me in the car, and Mauricio followed after Robert, making sure to catch him in case he fell. He walked slowly, hunched over with his cane. It took Robert a few minutes to slowly sit himself in the car and catch his breath.

As we walked into Alpha and Omega Church, two greeters opened the tinted glass doors, smiling and welcoming us. In the lobby, behind a glass wall was a bookstore where people were purchasing copies of the pastor's message. On the other side of the lobby was a concierge desk, like at a hotel, staffed by volunteers answering questions from newcomers. Behind the volunteers, a big-screen TV showed a middle-aged woman about fifteen years older than me, with wavy black hair and long ornate earrings. Following her was an older tanned man with a white beard and a broad smile that reached the crow's-feet in his eyes.

"He's the head pastor, Delgado. The lady is his wife, Mariam," Mauricio said, noticing my fixation on the screen.

Robert noticed the screen and recognized Pastor Delgado as well.

"He was with Joel Osteen when he was at a conference here in Miami! That's one of the local pastors he had onstage with him!" He paused for a minute and stayed silent.

Years of experience taught me to wait for the next phrase. He was like an old computer running on dial-up—expect lots of buffering.

"Well?" I shook my head. "Enough suspense! What happened at the conference?"

"When we were there, the Holy Spirit spoke to me. It told me to go to his church. He was fatter then, but it's the same face. This is crazy, man!"

We walked through another set of double doors into the main temple, which looked like a concert hall. There were two large screens on either side so everyone, no matter where they sat, could see the pastor. People were already coming in and taking their seats. I followed Robert toward the front, and he sat at the second row, in the seat closest to the aisle, in case we needed to make a quick escape to the car to breathe.

It was my first time in a Christian church, and although I'd been Catholic all my life, I didn't know what to expect. A band started playing the first song. The lights dimmed, and in tune with the singers, lyrics appeared on the screen.

*You give hope, You restore*
*Every heart that is broken*
*Great are You, Lord*

I looked at Robert. He had his eyes closed, so I closed mine too. I started praying for him, holding on to the words of the song.

*It's Your breath in our lungs*
*So we pour out our praise*
*We pour out our praise*
*It's Your breath in our lungs*
*So we pour out our praise to You only*

There was serenity in that moment. Through my closed eyes tears welled up and started running down my cheeks. In that moment, there was a space between the cancer and me. Until that moment, the cancer felt like it was clinging to our skin, present in every second. At least for this moment it was pulled back, and a presence unlike any I'd ever felt before was there. If it were allowed, I would have collapsed in my seat and cried my eyes out until I ran out of tears. Instead, that presence held me.

I know now that was God. And I know that first song was meant for us. We were exactly where we needed to be. Taking a moment, I moved past Robert and went back to the lobby to get tissues. I needed a minute to collect myself. While I was drying my eyes, I recognized the pastor's wife, Mariam. Followed by her assistant, she walked straight to me in the empty lobby.

"Are you okay?" she asked, putting her hand on my shoulder.

"My husband, Robert, was diagnosed with stage 4 lung cancer recently." Shaking, I couldn't get any more words out.

"Oh no!" she said firmly in a smoky voice with a thick Spanish accent.

"We're a cancer-free church. Close your eyes!"

Before I could say anything more, she had hers closed and was praying.

"Your Word says that by His stripes we are healed, Father. I declare healing over her husband's life. Cancer has no authority in his body, and we command it to leave. You have plans for life and not for death for this woman's husband! In the name of Jesus! Amen!"

It was over before I knew it. And just as quick, she encouraged me and left. I went back to Robert, who was still crying his eyes out, and so was Alicia.

After the worship, Pastor Delgado gave a sermon on faith. I was still processing what his wife had prayed for us, and I didn't catch everything in his message.

"It doesn't matter what you're going through! If God tells you something in His Word, just believe it, man! Don't try to figure it out—*that's* His job. Your job is to believe it!"

That I could hold on to! I squeezed Robert's hand tight.

He leaned over and whispered in my ear, "No matter how bad I get, I never want to miss another Sunday coming here."

I squeezed his hand tighter.

The next day, back at school, after the kids had gone to lunch and I had some time to myself, I pulled out Dodi Osteen's book to read some more. At the end of her book, she included a list of Bible scriptures for healing. I couldn't wait to share them with Robert when I got home. Then my phone rang.

"Hello?"

"Leila?" came Robert's voice.

"Hi, babe! Is everything okay?" I asked, my mind creating scenarios for his calling me out of the routine. He never called me at work, and now with cancer, you expect the worst from any surprise.

"Dr. Kaywin called me to go over the appointment for the port surgery. For chemo. In my last visit with him, he said that he wasn't sure which kind of chemo to give me. He was between regular chemo and Keytruda, another medicine he says works with your own immune system to kill the cancer."

"Uhuh."

"He says it takes less of a toll on your body. Well, anyways, he calls me all excited because the FDA just approved Keytruda and chemo to be given at the same time!"

"That's great, honey! So what does that mean?"

"I don't know, but if he's excited, it must be good news!"

"Tell me about the port surgery. What's the plan?" I asked, making sure there were no interruptions to the plan.

"I checked the calendar and confirmed with the hospital. It's going to be this Thursday, at 2:30 p.m. Mauricio and Alicia are going to go with me. Kaywin says the surgeon put the port in my chest so the medicine can go to the heart and it gets distributed to the rest of my body from there."

"Okay! Things are moving forward!"

"Yep."

"The plan is working!"

"Plan? What plan?"

"Never mind. Bye!"

"Leila, what plan?"

"The plan to get you better, Robert!"

"Oh." He giggled. "Yup."

"Love you."

After hanging up with him, I closed the book and thanked God for that moment yesterday in church, for the people He put in our lives to help us through this. For the first time since the diagnosis, I had hope.

The days until Thursday flew! But on Thursday, I could not get out of school fast enough. The whole day I had Robert on my mind: Would he get to the hospital on time? Would Alicia and Mauricio be with him to answer any questions he couldn't? I called Alicia a few times that day to confirm the details, but I was still nervous.

He was still losing weight and getting weaker by the day, and there was a concern in the meeting to go over the surgery, of him not being able to get it if he got too weak. After dismissing the kids to their parents, I got to my car as quick as I could to get to the hospital.

"Did they start yet?" I called Alicia.

"Yes, they just took him now," came her reply. "Maury went to get some lunch in the cafeteria for us, and he'll bring it back here to the waiting room."

"Keep me posted, please. Please!"

"Okay!"

It would be another hour stuck in traffic by the time I got to the waiting room a little before 4:00 p.m. I spotted Alicia behind her computer, seated at a little round coffee table, studying for her license exam. Mauricio next to her, reading a book.

"Have they said anything?" I asked, taking a seat next to them.

"A little while ago, the surgeon came out and said there was a complication."

I gripped my purse a little tighter.

"He said that they were trying to put the port in the chest but the vein they needed to use to get to his heart was too tight. What did he call it, babe?"

"He has SVC syndrome," said Alicia, not looking up from her computer.

"What does that mean? Alicia, can you look up and talk?"

"Mommy! It means the cancer is compressing his superior vena cava, one of the biggest veins in his chest. The surgeon said they were going to try another way, but he went back in and hasn't come out yet. We don't know anything else! Can you sit still?"

"No! I won't be okay until I know how he's doing. They were supposed to put it on his chest."

"Leila." Mauricio got up. "I'm going to bring you some tea from the cafeteria. You should eat something too. He's going to be fine."

"I can't eat until I know he's okay."

"I'm still bringing you that tea."

This wasn't part of the plan. It was supposed to be a quick procedure, an hour usually, an hour and a half tops, the doctor said. It had been over two and a half hours already. What could be taking so long? I kept looking at the clock, going over the plan in my head. It was the only thing that was supposed to make sense: follow the plan and he'd be okay. That was the deal, right? Now we were changing the plan, and I hated it!

Mauricio came back with the tea, and a nurse called us into the recovery area. I kept rubbing my hands together for warmth. Looking around every open curtain to find him, I wondered if he'd be asleep.

"Were they able to install the port?" I asked the nurse.

"Ma'am, the surgeon will be right out to answer your questions."

I heard him around the corner. Mauricio was walking in front of us, and I couldn't see past his back. I expected him to be screaming at somebody that they changed the location of the port.

"Hi, honeeeeyy!" he yelled, swaying his head from side to side, a goofy smile on his face. He waved to nurses and other patients like he was the Queen of England.

"You should know," said the nurse guiding us, "he's a little out of it from the anesthesia, but it will wear off in a few minutes."

"You don't say!"

"Look!" he said to me, all excited. "They gave me a South Beach shave!" Pulling off the front of his gown.

"Oh, good God, man!" said Mauricio, looking away. "Yup, can't unsee that now!"

"SPAPI!"

"Honey, close your legs!" I yelled, trying to keep a straight face. "You're showing your goods to everybody!"

"I done never had a South Beach shave before!" He kept looking at it, wide eyes and smiling from ear to ear. "I like it!"

"I'm sure you do, honey!" My sides hurt from laughing. "Settle down now!"

The orderlies transferred him to the bed, every one of them stifling a laugh at the show.

As I put a blanket over his legs, the surgeon pulled back the curtain. A tall muscular man in green scrubs looked at his vitals and explained, "We had to put the port in his leg. We could have gone through the chest, but with the superior vena cava syndrome, the vein was tighter than I would have liked, and that could have led to complications down the line."

"And it's okay in the leg?" I asked.

"Absolutely. We threaded it to another vein up to his heart. So now we'll look at his recovery for another hour, and then they'll send him home."

"And that won't delay chemotherapy?"

"No medical reason that it should. He's good to go!"

He excused himself, leaving us there looking at my husband, who was still high as a kite slowly coming back down to earth.

"Thank You, God!" I whispered, letting out a sigh of relief.

"Honey?" said Robert, slowly coming back to himself.

"Hi, handsome!" I smiled

"Heyyy, I made it okay?"

"You did just fine. Though you may have to apologize to Mauricio later."

"Uh-oh. What I do?" Shifting a little in bed, he lifted up the sheets and looked at me, brow furrowed. "Where is my underwear?"

# The Breaking Point

*Robert*

"You seriously don't remember after the surgery?" asked Mauricio.

"Not a thing," I said, cutting my french fry into pea-size pieces and stabbing them with a fork.

"Let's put it this way, man," he said, halfway through a ham sandwich. "You and I skipped a few levels of intimacy that day."

Leila snorted, choking on diet Coke. "I forgot about that!"

"I haven't!"

"Dude, I was so out of it I don't remember the recovery, going home, or much of yesterday. Except for this bump on my leg that I feel every time I move, it was most of a blur." I sipped my ice tea.

"How was the nutritionist appointment today?" asked Leila.

"Good," said Mauricio, going back to his sandwich.

"No. Not good! I'm a hundred and forty pounds!"

No one said anything. They didn't know what to say. For the last eight weeks, I'd been getting skinnier and weaker. I had lost the energy to oversee the jobs in person, leaving them to my supervisor. Every day since the operation, I would sit in the recliner and try to nap, to regain some strength. The constant pain from cancer digging into my chest and hip and the ball deforming my jaw made eating almost impossible.

"We'll take care of that," said Mauricio, breaking the silence. "Leila, do you mind if I cook dinner from now on? I want to help out."

"Yes! Yes, please!" Her eyes lit up. "It's always a fight trying to figure out dinner."

"Oh, thank God!" said Alicia. "Cantina was getting old!"

Her mother shot her a look.

"What did the nutritionist say?" asked Leila, changing the subject.

"Spapi needs to eat thirty five hundred calories a day *just* to maintain his current weight."

"Why?" she asked, dunking a french fry in ketchup.

"Cancer loves sugar. It's feeding on all the sugar in his body as it grows," said Mauricio, taking a bite of Alicia's steak sandwich.

"Hey! That's mine!"

It sounded like a joke. How would they expect me to eat that much food when I had zero appetite and I could only open my mouth far enough to grab a straw or chew a tiny bit of pancake?

"Given the situation with his jaw," she said, "a smoothie would probably be the best way to get nutrients into him."

"So we can make you a soft food diet to start," said Mauricio, grabbing a pen and paper. "It'll have to be a calorie bomb, lots of cream and butter. We can alternate between soft purees and the smoothies so you don't get bored so quickly."

"Ooh, butter! Yum!" said Leila, trying to sound enthusiastic.

"Yeah," said Alicia. "She said to eat dark leafy greens like kale, and lots of high-calorie stuff like ice cream and peanut butter."

*A kale, ice cream, and peanut butter smoothie? You can't be serious!*

"Let's try it, babe," said Leila. "I'll make it in the morning before work, and we can see how it goes."

That night, the ceiling in our bathroom swayed, catching the light of the pool outside. Eddies and ripples flowed over the towel rack and the palm tree paintings hanging on the walls, completing the tropical decor my wife designed for our bathroom. If only she were awake to see it! She, too, was bathed in ebbing light; her hair shone and faded, then shone again. Her snores matched the soft tempo, and for one moment, everything was in harmony. My eyes grew heavy, and I tried sleeping, rocked by my wife's steady, rhythmic snores. Then the pain started again. A rushing wave of agony pulsed through my hip, creeping up my spine. In short, quick breaths, I let it wash over me, making my eyes water.

I propped up another pillow on my back, sitting upright in bed and waiting for the attack to pass. Time between the waves got longer, but just when I thought I could catch sleep, another one began. I limped to the recliner in the living room, and here, too, was the bouncing light from the pool. I sank into the leather and curled up. This loosened pressure in my spine, and a wave of relief made its way down to my toes.

Every night was the same battle. I only remember small moments when I wasn't in pain. Every other moment in my life now had this debilitating anguish. It aged me, like I was born an old man, in constant pain, that needed to switch between a recliner and a bed every half-hour. If this were me, then the memories of picking huckleberries in South Carolina as a kid, of holding my children in my arms, and of making love to my wife happened to someone else. Not to me. I was always an old man with cancer.

Then, from another part of me rose a rebellious anger, like a man that had been beaten just one too many times. *When would this chemo start?* I pounded the armrest, barely making a thud into the soft leather.

With these feelings boiling in my gut, I went back to bed. At five fifteen, Leila got up, showered, and made me a pancake.

"I'm making you your smoothie so you can have it later. You'll remember to have it?"

"Yup," I said, nibbling a piece the size of a pea.

"You're sure?" She hoisted her workbag. "I'll leave it in the blender in the fridge."

"Uhuh."

It wasn't enough that I hadn't slept or that I was in constant hip pain; the mornings brought their own little hell. Standing upright in the mornings gave me a shooting pain in the chest, like knives sticking into it. So I hunched over, looking at the pancake and, when I walked, at the floor.

"And get your head out of your hands, please!" she said, exasperated. "None of that now. You're going to have a good day! Right?"

"Right, right. Yes…" *Or else.*

She put the blender full of brown sludge in the fridge, grabbed her bag, and kissed me, bolting for the door. It wasn't yet six in the morning, but I texted Dr. Juvenal about the pain. He did say in the diagnosis that whatever I needed, day or night, to text him, so I thought, *Here goes nothing.* Right? I told him my symptoms and the pain.

A few minutes later, I got a text!

*Does this guy not sleep?*

"It's probably heartburn from all the medication you're taking. Take Zantac."

"How much?"

"What it says on the box. If that doesn't work in thirty minutes, take more."

"Won't that affect me with the other medication you have me on?"

"You could take everything in your medicine cabinet and it wouldn't affect anything I have you on."

*That's reassuring.*

By nine, the pain was starting to go away. After two doses of Zantac and shuffling around the house to get my mind off the pain, I changed into work clothes and answered e-mails. The front door groaned open and slammed shut.

"I'm late!" yelled Alicia, running down the driveway to her car. By the time I walked to the living room to say good-bye, she was already down the street. Mauricio came out of his room dressed in one of my old company pools and jeans.

"You didn't hear? She's late!" He smiled.

"About time you got up!" I tossed him the keys to my truck. "You're driving me today."

"Good morning to you too, sunshine," he said, pushing my keys into his pockets.

We drove past groves of oak trees planted in the sixties, between mansions on either side, finally pulling into an asphalt driveway. Before I got off the car, Mauricio was already opening the door for me. Walking around the jobsite, he stood two steps behind me, probably in case I fell and he could catch me. Inside the house, my guys were busy installing impact windows. Already they had demolished most of the old house, taken it down to the studs, and installed new electrical wiring, plumbing, and drywall.

Before we left the house, I stopped him at the front door. I couldn't figure out how he came into our lives and why he fit in so well with us; there was this unnatural peace about him being with us. This kid came to town to be with my daughter, yet he was here making sure I could get around, keep my business. "Mauricio," I asked, "what are you doing for money?"

He stopped and looked around, hesitant for a second, trying to figure out how to answer.

"I'm working with my mom at our company. She started a business helping truckers, and I help her from my computer. While there are no cooking events, that's what I do to get by. Why?"

"No reason," I said. "Curious." I got into my truck.

He cranked the ignition.

New night, same pains. Same change from the bed to the recliner and back. Same pancake with syrup. Same kiss goodbye.

*God, please, something has to change!* I prayed, my head in my hands on the kitchen table.

After Alicia left for work, I went to the bathroom to pee, half-awake, my mouth dry from the medicine. It took me a full minute to realize the toilet bowl was full of bright-red blood.

*That's it! The cancer is in my kidneys!*

"Lord," I started praying out loud, "this means you've decided not to heal me and take me home?"

Time has a tendency to stand still when you think you're going to die. My breaths became shorter and faster as a wave of panic rushed over me. But if that was going to happen, I was going to do everything I could to leave my wife and kids taken care of. I left the bathroom and looked at Mauricio's door. Closed. He hadn't woken up yet. He and I were the only ones home, and I battled the urge to knock on his door. Many times I almost did, but something held me back. I paced the living room, wishing he would wake up already!

Then his door opened, and he headed for the bathroom.

"Good morning! Please come with me." I pulled him into the office. "Sit with me while I show you something."

"Okay, what's going on, Robert?"

I showed him the spreadsheets of jobs we had going, their stages of progress, and how to follow them to get payment from the clients to fund the jobs, do payroll, and give the profits to Leila. If I wasn't going to be around, I would need him to make sure my family was taken care of. I could tell he was lost; it was too much information for someone who had zero knowledge of construction, but he did not back away.

"Show it to me again," he said.

We did. The whole thing, from top to bottom. I showed him how to run the whole company. He sat quietly for a few moments, his eyes on the spreadsheets, digesting the information.

"Now, why are you showing me this?"

I rolled my chair to face him.

"You need to listen to me very carefully, and you can't say any of this to Alicia or Leila. They already have too much stress on them, and this will freak them out even more. So I need you."

He nodded. "Of course."

"This morning, I started peeing blood. I'm afraid this is it for me. If I'm peeing blood because the cancer spread to my kidneys, it might be soon. So just in case it is, I need you to look after them."

We stayed silent for a few minutes. It was a lot that I was asking of this kid. More than I had the right to ask for. But I had no one else.

"Well," he said, slapping his knees, "you're not dead yet. So God still has something for you to do here. Have you called the doctor?"

I called Juvenal, but he hadn't answered his phone this morning. I left a voice mail and was waiting for a call back. I looked at him, furrowed brow, questioning his reaction. "You're not freaking? I'm freaking, man!"

"Are we calling 911?"

"No. I want to hear from Juvenal first."

"Then I'm not freaking. I'm not leaving your side, though. But I'm not freaking."

We sat in the kitchen table in silence. By ten Juvenal called, and we went over the symptoms.

"From what you're telling me, it's probably a reaction to the antibiotics you're on. What is it, cephalexin?"

I looked at the bottle in the medicine cabinet.

"Yup."

"Stop taking them right now. My guess is you're probably allergic to them. Stop them and call me if you keep peeing blood today."

"Okay. Should I go to the hospital? I can have Mauricio take me right now."

"Just call me if you keep peeing blood. Let's go from there."

*Something changed, all right!*

Mauricio was eyeing some plans for one of the houses we were remodeling. "I can't read them."

I stood next to him.

"What am I looking at, Rob? You need to teach me everything you can. If something were to happen to you, I'd like to be helpful."

*He was right—I'm not dead yet.*

"You're looking at the structural plan. These are the exterior walls."

We spent the rest of the morning going over the plans. Explaining to him how to read them and see where the architect made comments for us to follow. I dropped a bomb on him this morning. But he didn't run away.

By lunchtime, I had peed already and, thank God, no blood. Mauricio made a sandwich, and I poured myself a glob of fresh brown smoothie Leila made that morning. It tasted as good as it looked, nutty, with an metallic tinge from the kale and some weird sweetness from the strawberries. It tasted like cancer would taste if they removed it from your body, blended it, and served it to you in a glass. Meanwhile, his sandwich was staring me in the face, ham, Swiss cheese, a dollop of mustard and mayo, and just enough lettuce. As far as I was concerned, it was the world's most perfect sandwich.

*I would kill for a bite of that sandwich. If I could bite anything.*

We worked until my sister Joyce called from South Carolina. Mauricio cleaned the notebooks and plans off the kitchen table while I sat in the recliner to talk to her.

"We want to go see you, Bobby!" came her voice over the speaker. "How have you been feeling?"

"I've been okay, Joyce. Don't come, though. It's not that bad."

"Isn't the cancer stage 4?"

"Yes, but it's little!" I lied. "Really, don't bother yourself about it. I'll have you come see me in a few weeks after the chemo so we can spend some time together."

I really didn't want them to see me. Leila and I found out quickly that whenever anyone tells anyone about cancer in general, their face changes to pity, their voice softens, and they try to be sympathetic. You are no longer you; now you're a fragile version of that person, who can break if not handled carefully. "I'm still me!" I wanted to yell at them. But they couldn't help it. So the fewer people know about the cancer, the better.

That evening, after dinner and the kids went to their rooms, I sat Leila on the bed and told her the watered-down version of the blood in the urine.

"Juvenal says it's not a big deal." *Liar!*

"Oh my god!" she yelled, her eyes wide, crossing her arms.

"It hasn't happened again." *That was true.*

"Oh my god, babe!"

"Baby, I'm okay!" *C'mon, dude, who are you kidding?*

She hugged me tight, and I wiped the tears that were forming in her hazel eyes. Then anger set in.

"And you didn't think to tell me?" She punched my shoulder. "I'm your wife! You tell me these things!"

Thank God it was Friday and she did not have school the next day, because with these news I pretty much made sure she wouldn't be sleeping that night.

The night pains came again, changing from the bed to the recliner—only this time they also brought another symptom. A casual reminder that I was living with something inside me that was living also and spreading and changing, and when you thought you were used to how things were, it changed on you.

I couldn't catch my breath. I switched back and forth between the recliner and the bed, and by the third time I walked in the room, Leila was already awake and out of bed. It was 2:00 a.m.

"Robert, what are we going to do?" she said, putting her hand on my forehead, feeling for a fever. "You're not sleeping. I'm not sleeping. Do I call 911?"

I sat on the bed, trying to catch my breath for a few minutes. Nothing.

"Call them."

She dialed the phone and woke Alicia up. By the time paramedics got to the house, everyone was awake and dressed to go. They monitored my vitals, put an IV port on my arm and an oxygen cannula in my nostrils.

"Yeah, we have to go to the ER," said the young paramedic reading my vitals in his monitor. He motioned to his partner. "Bring the stretcher."

"What's the official cause?" asked Alicia, arms crossed.

"Respiratory distress."

They loaded me into the ambulance and started driving down my street. Leila was in the back with me and one of the paramedics.

"Okay, Mr. Germroth, we're taking you to the closest hospital, which is Kendall Regional—"

"NO!" said Leila and I in unison.

"He's a cancer patient. He needs to go to Baptist Hospital."

"Ma'am, I assure you," said the lead paramedic, who was in the passenger seat up front, "they'll take very good care of him there—"

"I'm sorry, NO!" said Leila again. "All his medical records are at Baptist. That's where you're taking him."

"Ma'am, by law we're required to take him to the closest hospital."

"Let me put it this way," I said, between breaths, "either you take me to Baptist Hospital or I'm getting off at the next stop sign and my wife can drive me there."

The lead paramedic sighed, shrugged, and nodded to the driver.

"Sir, we'll take you to Baptist Hospital. Just calm down."

The paramedics took me off the ambulance and sat me on a wheelchair in the passenger drop-off area. Like clockwork, a nurse took the medical information from the paramedics and gave me an oxygen mask so I could breathe better. Leila was walking ahead, trying to get her bearings, finding a landmark where to tell the kids to join us.

"Mr. Germroth," said the nurse, a young brunette not much older than Alicia. "Hang tight, we're going to get to you as soon as we can."

"He's a cancer patient!" said Leila. "He was supposed to have his first chemo tomorrow. That will still happen, right?"

"The doctor will know more, ma'am," she said, holding on to her clipboard. "Follow me, please." She guided us to the main lobby, and we waited.

"How's he feeling?" came Alicia's voice, Mauricio trailing behind her, fighting a yawn.

Leila brought them up to speed. Mauricio knelt down in front of my wheelchair and patted the back of my hand.

"You're going to be okay."

An hour passed, and it was just the four of us in the waiting room. Everyone else had been called.

"Ger-mruth?" -called a nurse, opening the door to the exam area.

*Hard* G. *Like* germ, *please.*

"That's us!" yelled Leila, raising her hand to get the nurse's attention.

They wheeled us to an examination room and brought a patient gown that only covered the front. "Let's get you on the bed," said the nurse. "The doctor will be with you in a moment." She took my temperature and hooked me up to the monitors.

More waiting.

Leila and Alicia fell asleep on the chairs beside my bed. Mauricio was watching the TV in the corner. He didn't move, keeping his shoulder fixed as Alicia's pillow. After an hour, another nurse came in and looked at the monitors.

"Mr. Germroth," she started, "according to this monitor, your oxygen saturation is good. Pulse is normal. Everything looks good."

"But I still can't breathe."

She drew some blood. "We'll run some tests and get back to you."

Around four in the morning, the doctor finally came, a handsome young Asian man who was probably in his early thirties.

"Mr. Germroth," now he started, "according to the monitors, you're fine." Sounding chipper. "What's going on?"

"Another nurse said the same thing! But no one is looking at me. Stop looking at the stupid monitors and listen to the patient!" I felt myself screaming. Leila and Alicia woke up.

The doctor didn't flinch. "Absolutely! Lean forward for me, please." With his stethoscope he listened to my lungs and took my temperature again. He signaled for my nurse. "Let me take a look at the labs when they come in. Something's wrong here."

His hospital phone beeped. Reading the alert, he turned to us. "I'll be right back."

A few minutes later, he came in with a male nurse carrying a syringe sealed in a package.

"Sorry for the wait, Mr. Germroth, but I have your results. You seem to have pneumonia caused by an infection in your right lung. I heard a fluid buildup, which is probably the cause of the pneumonia. I know you're a cancer patient, so we'll have to take care of this infection first before you can have any chemotherapy."

*So much for having it tomorrow.*

Leila threw her head back. "Isn't there anything you can do?" she asked. I could hear the desperation in her voice. "He needs this chemotherapy! He's been in pain for weeks, and the cancer just keeps growing!"

"Ma'am," said the doctor, holding up his hands in the most reassuring tone he could muster. "I hear you. You have to understand that chemotherapy destroys a person's immune system. If he has any infection and still gets his chemo, there is nothing stopping that infection. It runs through the body like wildfire and will kill the patient."

*I'm right here!*

"We're admitting him for the pneumonia, and I will reach out to the oncologist on his case. He will determine when you're ready for chemo. Right now we're just waiting for a room to become available so we can move you from here."

*Don't worry, Doctor, I'm patient.*

"Mr. Germroth, we're giving you now a shot of steroids to open up your lungs. This should help you breathe better."

The nurse sat by my bed and injected the liquid from the needle into my IV. Almost immediately, I was able to breathe deep, my lungs opened, and my breathing slowed down to normal.

"We'll come get you when a room becomes available," said the doctor again, and both left the room, turning off the lights so I could sleep. I sank my head into the pillow, feeling relief for the first time that night.

"You guys go home. Get some sleep."

"We can stay. It's not a problem."

"No." Leila was adamant, wrapping herself in a white hospital blanket to keep out the cold. "I'll stay with him, then you can come back after you get some sleep."

After some tired protest from both of them, they left, promising to be back in the afternoon.

At 10:00 a.m., we were finally given a room on the fourth floor. Although it was larger than the examination room back in the ER, the decoration was pulled straight from the eighties, which was probably the last time anyone did work on this hospital floor. Sanded beige wallpaper met lime-green floor tile in a jagged triangle pattern. Every piece of backboard, headboard, and door trim was lined with varnished brown wood. Whatever the decorations, I was glad for a bed and a recliner for Leila—we were both exhausted.

After the admitting doctor introduced himself and confirmed the pneumonia, he prescribed oxycodone every four hours for the pain. Our new nurse, Jessica, brought the first dosage around eleven. Even with oxycodone, it only dulled the pain, but it was enough that, for the first time in months, I had a really deep sleep.

"Mr. Germroth?"

My eyes adjusted to the light; three blurry shapes huddled together at the foot of my bed.

"Mr. Germroth!"

"Good to see you, Robert," said the soft voice of the man in the center.

"Dr. Kaywin!" I slurred, still groggy from the medication. "I'm still here!"

"Yes, you are!" He smiled. "I asked Dr. Barrios and Dr. Martinez to be here with me so we can all be on the same page regarding your treatment."

Barrios walked to my side, pulled our his stethoscope, and listened to my chest and lungs.

"Now that you're in the hospital because of an infection, we are going to run tests to see how much the cancer has progressed, and the extent of the infection," said Kaywin.

"Okay."

"Will he still be able to get chemo soon?" interrupted Leila.

Kaywin held up his hand to stop her.

*I know that gesture. Uh-oh.*

"If we give him the chemo now, with an infection in his system, it's like taking a loaded gun and killing him. Chemo kills all the white blood cells in the body that help fight infection. So our first task is to control that infection."

"Yeah, the ER doctor told us this morning."

"Right," Kaywin continued. "I also don't like giving chemo, especially the first time, in the hospital. Your immune system is already trying to recover, and there is a lot of bacteria here, which could give you another infection quickly. We're going to have to move you to the oncology floor as soon as a bed becomes available before we can give you chemo."

Leila had her arms crossed, her eyes steeled on Dr. Kaywin, taking in his words.

"I'm going to have a team of doctors come see you so we can proceed, so just wait for them and I'll wait for their results."

*Great.*

Around 3:00 p.m., the cardiologist came in, introduced himself, took a look at my chart, and asked me to tell him the story.

"Uhuh, uhuh...stage 4...no chemo yet...infection in lungs," he said without looking up from his chart. "I'm going to order a CT and MRI, and we'll go from there."

"Okay, thanks."

"Feel better, Mr. Jermroth," he said, walking out the door.

*Isn't that what you're here for?*

Not long after, another doctor showed up. This one in a lab coat, green tie, and purple dress shirt. He introduced himself as the nephrologist. Leila was in the recliner next to me, same stonewall face.

"I'm the kidney doctor, Mr. Germroth. Would you turn to your side for me?" He listened to my lungs and felt around my kidneys.

"Can you go through the story with me?"

"Again? Don't you guys talk to one another? Don't you guys talk to Kaywin?"

"We do." He pressed down on a kidney. "But I like to get it from the patient myself."

So we went over the whole thing again. Stage 4; cancer in lung, brain, jaw, hip, spine; no sleeping for weeks; constant pain; and yes, I peed blood.

"I'm going to order an ultrasound for your kidneys. I want to make sure the cancer hasn't spread there and that the only reason you urinated blood was an allergic reaction to an antibiotic."

I nodded.

"Hang tight, okay?" He left the room.

The same thing happened with the neurologist, liver doctor, radiologist, infectious disease doctor, and the psychiatrist, who offered to prescribe antianxiety meds right away. With each new doctor, Leila grew increasingly annoyed. We felt like monkeys at the zoo, just another attraction in the show. I knew her mind; we'd been in the hospital a whole night and day already, and nothing but interviews had happened. Interviews and scheduled tests, and every test so far had revealed that the cancer had progressed, I was getting sicker, and no one was doing anything about it. Twenty-two years of marriage don't happen without learning how to read your wife.

By 7:00 p.m., the head of facial reconstruction surgery showed up. This was the guy that people requested to have their faces rebuilt after a disfiguring accident, according to the nurses. With my face how it was, misshapen and twisted from the cancer, Kaywin asked him to see me.

He went over the story again. Cancer...blah, blah, blah...stage 4...no cure.

*Heard that.*

Then the analysis, say "Aahahh," and jamming a probe stick down my throat.

"Yeah." He shook his head. "Once the cancer gets in the jawbone, the patient is a goner."

*I'm. Right.* HERE!

Leila got up, grabbed my hand, and looked at the doctor straight in the eyes.

"But with God, everything is possible."

"Absolutely!" he said, not looking up from his clipboard. "I don't want to operate now with the jaw as it is. I'd rather wait a few months to see how the cancer progresses before we talk about operating on the bone. I'll have a nurse schedule a follow-up in a few months."

He turned around and walked out of the room. "Best of luck, Mr. Germroth."

For the next half-hour, Leila paced back and forth in front of my bed, fuming at this doctor's bedside manner.

"And he has the nerve to tell us, in front of *you*, that you're a goner in six months! Are you kidding me? And did you see his face when I told him that with God anything was possible? He might have called me a lunatic to my face!"

I coughed and grabbed the oxygen mask, putting it over my mouth. You learn that, too, as a husband, silence can save your life.

"If one more doctor shows up today, I'm *losing* it!" she said, finally sitting back down.

After a soft knock on the door, in walked a petite brunette in a lab coat and a messy bun on her head.

"Hi, I'm the nutritionist. Dr. Kaywin asked me to speak with you!"

Leila stopped cold. Eyes locked on mine, big as saucers. I tried to stifle the laughter, but with the mask on, it actually caused a coughing fit. Saliva was flying from the openings in the mask as I laughed and coughed at my wife's reaction.

"Is this Mr. Je-erm-Roth?"

"Yes!" I nodded, slapping my thigh. *Cough, cough.* "Come in!"

"I'll go for a walk. You can talk to her!" said Leila, storming out of the room.

"Hard *G*, dear. Like *grape*. Yes."

*Every time.*

# Take Me Home

*Robert*

"I'm not hungry."

"You need to eat, Robert! The nutritionist says you're too skinny! You're barely eating, and the cancer is eating you alive."

*I know. I know!*

I got used to doctors coming in, taking a look at me, and bringing more bad news. Leila, not so much. She was still sticking to the plan: "Get Robert to chemo and all will be well." Like I was some football you could just crash into the end zone and everything would be okay.

This morning I was already taken to an MRI then, at eleven, had my head and chest x-rayed. Before the day would be over, I would have more tests done. But for now the morning tests were done and the second round of pain meds, which I got with lunch, would kick in any minute.

Wearing my jean shorts under my hospital gown, I stared at the plate of chicken and rice sitting on my tray. Flecks of parsley dotted the meat and made it look like a plastic toy version of what chicken should look like. At least the other items on my tray were exactly where they were supposed to be, napkins on the upper right corner, water pitcher on the upper left, cell phone at bottom right, where I could get to it quickest, and my glasses exactly next to it. At least this felt right.

Leila came over to my side of the bed. She wasn't done arguing. Slowly I took a bit of rice on the fork and put it to my mouth. God, if hospitals are where you go because you want to live, why do they make hospital food that makes you want to die?

"Eat, Robert, please," pleaded Leila. "Here, I'll help you cut that chicken."

She took the fork and knife from my hands and started to run the knife through the chicken. I saw rice splatter on her face before I heard myself.

"Don't you touch my tray, woman!"

She backed away, slowly.

"Leave everything where it is. Don't touch *a thing*!"

She placed the knife and fork slowly back down. She reached into her purse, pulling out a handful of tissues and her wallet.

"I'll get some coffee," she said, wiping her face on her way out. After she left, a transporter came in.

"Mr. Germroth!" he said. "I'm here to take you to Imaging. We have an opening for you."

"Okay."

"Do you want me to wait for your wife? I just passed her in the hall."

"No, let's go."

I put the lid on lunch. At least I gave the cancer a fair shot at killing me; this chicken certainly would have.

"Will you have someone tell my wife you're taking me?"

"I'll inform the nurse to be on the lookout for her."

At Imaging, a technician had me lift up my shirt and then poured a gel down my back.

"Okay, Mr. Germroth, I'm going to apply the wand over your lung and you'll see on-screen what we're looking at."

"And what *are* we looking at?" I asked, gripping the edge of the mattress.

"We're doing an ultrasound to see where there is fluid in your lung. Dr. Barrios scheduled a thoracentesis when you first came in, so now we're going to see the fluid, and later we'll do the procedure."

"Thora-what?"

"Thoracentesis. Essentially, we're going to drain the fluid that's in your lungs that's preventing you to breathe normally."

"And just *how* do you drain that fluid?" My knuckles turned white from gripping the bed, and I wished Leila were here to hold my hand.

"We take a needle about six inches long and insert it between your ribs into the lower part of your lungs, where the fluid is, then drain it into this bottle."

*Yup. Already hate that answer!*

"Okay..."

"You won't feel any pain, just some pressure."

"You sure?" I tried to take a deep breath, but the pressure in my lungs felt like I had a car parked on my chest.

"Positive." He tried to sound reassuring, patting my shoulder. "We're done. I got the scans I needed and will be sending them to Dr. Barrios. After that, they'll do the thoracentesis. Just hang in there."

Another transporter wheeled me back into my room. Leila was back, this time with Mauricio and Alicia. She was reading a novel in the recliner, while Alicia rifled through her nursing school notes.

"Don't touch his tray," said Leila to Alicia dryly, not looking up from her book.

"I'm sorry," was all I could muster.

The afternoon passed in silence. Leila kept to herself in her lesson plans, school was ending any day, and she was busier than ever with her students. I tried to keep myself busy with work to take my mind off the impossibly long needle that was going to go into my back.

"Mauricio," I started, "bring me the papers I asked you from my office. I'm going to have you go to the jobsite, ask for Eddie, and report back to me how the construction is going."

From his bag he pulled what I asked for. I handed him back the papers and checks from Leila's purse. The guys would need to be paid for the week, and I wouldn't be there to do it. So Mauricio would have to. After getting the address of the jobsite, he got the checks, kissed Alicia, and headed for the door.

"And no lollygagging! Hurry up, or they'll leave for the day and you'll miss them."

"I got it, I got it!" he yelled, rushing for the elevator.

"Robert, do you see yourself?" asked Leila. "You're rude and nasty to people! To me, to your daughter, to that young man that's helping your business in ways that none of us could. You could be nicer. Say 'Thank you,' at least!"

"Thank you," I grumbled.

*Giant needle in my back. It's going to hurt like hell. And I'm already in so much pain. And they don't see that. Be nice? Try being without pain for ten seconds!*

In the evening, Leila went home to shower and change clothes. Every day since I got here, she would stay the night and the day and leave only for an hour to bathe and change. Now tomorrow was Monday, so she needed to bring clothes for work as well, since she was leaving for school straight from here. Alicia was watching me, and Mauricio was stuck in traffic on the way back. "Watching me" was exaggerated; she was watching the back of her eyelids in the recliner. Softly, the night nurse came in to introduce herself.

"So I hear you're having trouble with the thoracentesis," she said, smiling.

"A little," I lied. "That has to hurt a lot, and I'm already in so much pain from everything else. I'm not sure I could handle it."

"Well," she said, "God doesn't give us more than we can handle. I'm not saying it won't be pain-free, but they'll give you something to numb the skin and you'll be okay. I've had patients that had it. They've never complained of the pain."

"I'm just worn-out." I sighed. "I feel like I've lost control of my life."

She held out her hands and grabbed mine. "Don't lose faith. You believe in God, then you must believe what the Bible says, 'By His stripes we are healed.' Right?"

"That's right."

She squeezed my hands.

"Jesus went through worse for us."

Hearing her talk about God eased the fears of tomorrow. For that moment, I felt God's presence in the room; He had not forgotten me. She gave me the nighttime medication in a little disposable cup.

"I'll be back to check on you in a few hours." And she left.

Leila came back with Mauricio, and they found each other in the lobby. Quietly, Mauricio grabbed Alicia's books and took her home for the night. Leila squeezed my hand and took her place in the recliner. We kissed, and she read me Joyce Meyer's book on divine healing.

"'Oh my Lord, I cried unto thee, and thou has healed me,'" said Leila. "That was from Psalm 30."

I closed my eyes. "That's good."

She continued, "'Surely he took up our pain and bore our suffering, yet we considered him punished by God, stricken by him, and afflicted. But he was pierced for our transgressions, he was crushed for our iniquities; the punishment that brought us peace was on him, and by his wounds we are healed.' That's from Isaiah."

Her voice was trailing farther and farther away, and a warmth from the medication traveled from my toes up to my chest, easing the pains in my hips, spine, and chest.

"Leila?"

"Yes, honey?"

"I'm sorry about today."

"I know."

"I love you."

"I love you more."

The next morning, Leila had gone to work around 5:00 a.m. Alicia was at home, studying for her board certification, and while I poured honey over breakfast pancakes, the psychologist came to check in. The nurses overheard me screaming at Leila yesterday and requested he pay a visit. Gently he took a seat beside me and pointed to the tray in front of me.

"The reason you're snapping at people who touch your tray is simple: you're a guy that's always had his own business. You've always been the boss, taking control of situations and making them work. Now, nothing is in your control anymore. You go where they take you, feed you what you have to eat, not what you choose to eat, and you have this cancer dictating your every decision. So this tray, with all these items perfectly placed in the order you arranged them, is your way of keeping something in your control."

I looked down at the tray. It made sense. But I hated that he was right. It made the reality of living with cancer that much more real. Yet another thing that cancer took over without me realizing it.

*This is what I've been reduced to?*

"What you have to understand, Robert, is that you do have control. You can control how you react, and when you feel the fear or the anxiety building up, you can control it without lashing out at the ones you love."

"How?"

"Breathe," he said calmly, like it was the simplest thing in the world, leaning back on the recliner. "Take deep breaths in and out. If you're breathing, you ain't dying. Remember that."

That took me back to that song I first heard in church.

*It's Your breath in our lungs*
*So we pour out our praise to You only*

*I could do that.*

By the afternoon, just as I was ready to eat my lunch, this time tilapia and mashed potatoes, the same transporter showed up.

"This one doesn't look too bad, John. Do I have to go right now?"

"I'm afraid so, Robert. They're waiting on you," Replied the tall handsome black man in lime-green scrubs who got so good at wheeling me around the hospital.

"We got to stop making this a habit," I said, shaking my head and closing the lid on the plate.

We went past patient rooms and into the elevator for the procedure floor. My stomach twisted in knots as we got closer to the procedure room.

*Breathe. Just breathe.*

I closed my eyes and remembered the conversation with the nurse last night, taking a deep breath.

*Lord, you're giving me this, so that means I can handle it. Please see me through it. Amen.*

My hands were shaking by the time they got me on the procedure table. The doctor who was performing the thoracentesis was seated, waiting for me, tools at the ready. Just like in the ultrasound, he opened the back of my gown and poured the same cold gel that raises every hair in your body.

"Okay, Mr. Germroth, I found the fluid in your lungs," he said, looking at the monitor next to him. "I'm going to give you a small injection to numb the area, and then we'll drain."

"Okay..."

*Just breathe, Robert. Hee hee hooo, hee hee hoo...*

A small pinch later, it was okay. "That wasn't too bad."

"Now, you're going to feel some pressure, but not too much discomfort."

When it happened, it felt like someone had been jabbing at my ribs for hours, then inside me, I felt *things* moving in one direction: skin, tissue, muscle, and organs being pulled inward by the needle.

"Whops, I missed!" He chuckled. "Let me take a look at the scan again."

*What!*

"Let's try this again." He pulled out the needle and, I could swear, half my organs out with it.

"You've got to be kidding, man."

"This is normal! You're okay," he reassured me. "Deep breath?"

He went in again, same pressure, same pull, only now I felt a warm trickle down my back. Where he inserted the needle, he attached a hose to drain into a plastic container next to me. I could see the container slowly fill with an amber fluid that looked like a mixture of water and blood. Slowly the liquid in the jar climbed higher. And the higher it went up, the better I breathed.

"Six hundred milliliters! Mr. Germroth, you had basically three cups of liquid in your lungs. You must be breathing better now!"

I had forgotten how good it was to breathe freely. I straightened up, inhaled, and felt oxygen reach the deepest part of my chest. "Like it's my first breath..."

*Just breathe.*

Back in the room, I forced myself to eat the tilapia and mashed potatoes, now cold and stale. Alicia and Mauricio were already there, waiting for me. The nurse had filled them in on the procedure and how it went. She was seated with her legs on the chair, cradling a thick nursing book, and her head in her hands.

"How's it going?"

Mauricio, behind her, opened his eyes wide and shook his head. Bad question.

"I'm freaking out!" She looked up. "The test is in a month, and I have all this book to memorize, and two others. And the worst part is that the review course I'm taking, I can't watch from the hospital!"

I looked at Mauricio, pleading for help with my eyes so Alicia couldn't notice.

"Have you gone to the jobsite today?"

"No! I didn't know you needed me to go."

"Well, if I can't go, you have to be my eyes and ears in that place. It's your job now."

"Robert, I don't mind, but you realize I know nothing about construction, right?"

"Didn't stop you before. Go and let me know how they're doing."

After he left, Alicia and I stayed in the room by ourselves. She kept muttering to herself and furiously scribbled notes in her notebook. I went on my phone to check whatever e-mails I could answer from the hospital bed.

"Spapi, I'm surprised at you," said Alicia without looking from her notes.

"Uh-oh, why?"

"Ever since I remember, you wouldn't let anyone near your jobs—you wouldn't take a day off. You worked Sunday to Sunday because nobody else knew what they were doing without you there. Now you're asking Maury, who tells you he knows nothing about construction, and you're basically having him run your business for you while you're here. How come?"

I thought about it for a while. She was right, of course, but I didn't know why either. It felt seamless, if you could call it that. Ever since that kid came into our lives, him moving in, me showing him the business accounts, making him supervise my construction jobs, they all felt like the obvious thing to do, like there was no other choice that made sense.

"I don't know, Alicia. I just felt a peace about it. In every conversation we've had, he's been man enough to be up front about everything. Whatever I asked him, he told me the truth. Not like your ex, who got angry I called him a boy one time, when I was trying to help him out."

Alicia sighed, not looking up from her book. "Just be nice to him, please. I want to keep him."

"Oh yeah! Don't lose this one."

The next morning, Dr. Kaywin came by to check on me. Leila had gone to school early from the hospital, so I was alone, with instructions to text her everything the doctor said. He monitored my vitals and listened to my lungs.

"In the last five days you've been in the hospital, we've been able take care of the pneumonia. With the thoracentesis, you've been breathing better too, so that's good."

"That's great news, Dr. Kaywin. So when can we schedule chemo?"

"Not so fast. You've been here for almost a week, and we just got the pneumonia under control. We're still waiting on a room at the fifth floor. There's none available now. Also, I want you to start taking walks around this floor. You need to be as strong as possible by the time we start with chemo, and you've been lying in a bed for a long time. Studies show that the longer a patient stays in bed, the more the muscles atrophy and weaken, which takes months to recover."

*C'mon, man! Good news, but not good enough.*

"Another thing, I just listened to your lungs, and I hear a little bit of fluid in the right lung again. According to the latest scans, the mass on the right lung is so big that air and moisture get trapped underneath in, and that's what's causing the infection. I don't know why you're getting another fluid buildup so fast. I'll have to consult with the pulmonologist and see. But if this continues, we may have to do another thoracentesis."

"Are you kidding me?"

"I wish I were, Robert. We're trying to get you strong enough for chemo, but we have to take care of these issues first."

I stopped paying much attention after that. When he left, I texted Leila and filled her in.

How do we keep the faith when there's no progress to hold on to? I was dying, and I felt like I was dying in slow motion. First, the pain that wrecks your body, then your lungs trap infection, and to top things off, they tell you that you need to be rid of the infection before pumping your body full of poison to kill the cancer before it kills you. And it's not like procedures help much; each comes at a cost. You may breathe better from a thoracentesis at the cost of having a giant needle invade the innermost part of you.

*Lord, what do You want? Are You taking me home or keeping me here? And if so, why? I surrendered everything to You. What is Your plan for my life? Please, let me hear You. Talk to me!*

God stayed quiet.

That afternoon, after Leila got out of school, a nurse came in, one I hadn't seen before, with short hair and lime-green scrubs.

"Mr. Jerm-roth?" she asked

*I stopped fighting it.*

"That's me. What's up?"

"We have you scheduled for a swallow test. I'm here to take you up."

In a procedure room, the nurse helped me sit in a machine with what looked like a TV monitor by my head. There was no screen on it, just white plastic.

"That's the x-ray," said the nurse, seeing me trying to figure it out. "I'm going to give you barium to swallow, and the x-ray will show us how you're swallowing."

"Why do I need this?"

"Dr. Barrios believes that because of the cancer in your jaw and your difficulty swallowing, your lung is filling up with fluid. When you drink water, instead of it going down the esophagus to the stomach, part of it is going to your lungs. This test will help us determine that better."

She handed me a disposable cup with the liquid. It had the same consistency as water but tasted like a chalkboard.

"We're going to need to repeat a few times to confirm," she said, handing me another cup.

That evening, when the meals were brought in, next to the chicken, carrots, and peas was a little container of transparent goop. As Leila and I were trying to figure out what the heck it was, our daytime nurse came in to check on us before she left for the day.

"Oh, good! You got the honey-thick water!" she said excitedly.

"The what now?"

"Yeah! So it's water that's thickened so you can drink it and it doesn't go down to your lungs. The nurse that did your swallow test added it to your chart."

I spooned a bit and lifted it up to my face; the dang thing left a trail all the way back to the container!

"Robert, you're making a mess!" yelled Leila, picking up a bunch of napkins from my tray.

DON'T TOUCH MY—*Breathe...breeaaaathee.*

"Thank you, babe," I said as she wiped my chin, tray, and gown.

I grabbed the whole container and took a sip. It didn't taste like anything, but it felt like a cold loogie, and Leila could see it on my face.

"It's good."

*Liar!*

"I'll just drink it later."

By 7:00 p.m., Alicia and Mauricio had come to visit and relieve Leila so she could go home and shower. They had just walked in the door, and Leila was catching them up to the events of today.

"Any word on a room at the fifth floor?" asked Alicia.

"Still nothing," answered Leila, slinging her purse over her shoulder. "I've been keeping it quiet, but I'm ready to yell at somebody. It's been over a week already, and every day it's the same answer: 'Waiting for a room to become available.'"

"Mauricio!" I yelled, as he was about to sit on the chair in the corner of the room. "You're not doing anything. Go get the nurse and ask her when I'm being transferred."

"Spapi! Leave him alone!" snapped Alicia, getting more defensive of him.

Too late—he was already out the door.

"Robert! Be nice to the guy!" snapped Leila too.

It was fun to see them get so defensive of him, and getting them riled up kept me from thinking about cancer. But by the scowls on their faces, clearly they weren't amused. Leila picked up her pink sweater and her class binders and went home.

Mauricio was gone for a longer time than usual, but before I could ask Alicia to give him a call, he burst through the door out of breath; I could see his face flushed and his chest rising and falling under his blue flannel shirt.

"Tomorrow!" he said between gasps. "I had to find your nurse, who had to call the fifth floor, who had to call the nurse that was discharging a patient, and that took too long, so I ran up the stairs, found the nurse myself, and had her check the system. Then ran back down. Did I mention they're moving you tomorrow?"

"All right!" I threw my fists up in the air to celebrate, and the jabbing pain at my elbow reminded me I had an IV needle still in my arm. Monitors, alarms started beeping behind me.

"Spapi! You blew your IV," said Alicia, getting up from her chair to check my arm.

"How do you know?"

"Because I just finished graduating nursing school a month ago, that's why! Now stay still." She started adjusting the hoses and pushing buttons in the computer.

"No! Wait for a nurse to do it."

"I *am* a nurse. Just sit still!"

"I want my Baptist nurse to do it, not my daughter nurse!"

She rolled her eyes. "You realize I'm applying for jobs right *here* in this hospital now, right? Any moment now I'll *be* a Baptist nurse!"

"But you're not yet! Now, I want my nurse! Mauricio, go get the nurse!"

"Again?" he said, looking from the door. He sighed and disappeared.

"Dang, you are stubborn!" yelled Alicia in exasperation. "Fine!"

She sat back down. Monitors still beeping.

*Breathe, Robert, breathe.*

Because of the monitors and Alicia's stubbornness, I didn't notice a stabbing pain in my kidneys. The last time I felt something similar, I was peeing blood. Doubt and fear started creeping in again. My mind jumped at alert. Would there be another emergency? Would I start peeing blood again? We finally received news of finally going to the fifth floor, and now this kidney pain could delay all that. Suddenly, I went back to feeling naked and small, losing the progress we had made this week.

*Lord? Are you there?* I prayed.

"Okay! I'm here!" shouted Leila, bursting into the room, smelling of lilacs. She was wearing yoga pants and a Miami Dolphin's T-shirt. Behind her came the nurse, who turned off the monitors and fixed my IV. Leila already knew all about the fifth floor tomorrow, and it was the first time a smile broke her face.

Throughout that night, the pain in my kidneys kept getting more frequent, and when the night nurse came to bring medication at two in the morning, I asked her for a plastic urinal so I could pee without going to the bathroom.

I kept looking down at the plastic bottle to confirm what I was afraid of. An empty bladder and the warm red fluid in the urinal confirmed my suspicions.

The nurse and I locked eyes. She saw the fear in mine.

"I'll get the doctor."

"Thank you," I said quietly, to not wake up Leila.

No more sleep that night. While waiting for the doctor, or nurse, I stared at the ceiling, hoping for some sign from God that it was going to be okay.

Dawn rolled around, and Dr. Kaywin came in, already aware of the situation, because the kidney doctor followed him into the room. They looked at my vitals, looked at me, and the kidney doctor ordered blood work and a kidney ultrasound to rule out possible causes. Leila hated that I didn't wake her up when it happened.

"Don't worry, Robert," said Kaywin, trying to reassure me. "We'll figure this out—"

"Is this going to stop him from moving to the fifth floor?" asked Leila before he could finish.

"We'll see what the kidney tests show." Kaywin turned to the kidney doctor. "Schedule every tests you need ASAP. This is your first priority."

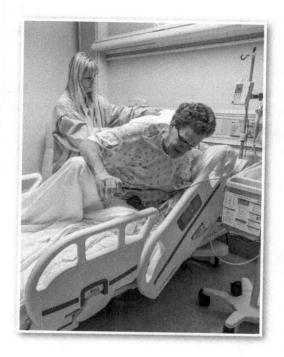

"Right away, Doctor," replied the kidney doctor.

They both left. I was amazed how much authority Kaywin carried, being one of the founding members of MCI; he really went the extra mile for his patients. At that moment, I really thanked God for Kaywin in my corner.

A few minutes later, the morning nurse came into the room and drew blood for lab work. "Someone will be here to pick you up for the kidney ultrasound soon," said the nurse, capping and labeling the filled vials. Maybe it was because of Kaywin, or something was really, *really* wrong, but everyone seemed to be in a rush around us.

An hour passed. Then two. Leila and I didn't speak; we just held hands. At the third hour, a transporter came in with a gurney. They took me to another procedure room, where a technician had me lift up my gown and poured the familiar cold gel on my lower back. "Stay still, Mr. Germroth. This should take fifteen minutes, and then we'll have you back in your room."

He applied the ultrasound wand at my left kidney, and the pressure started building. He kept pressing up and down, up and down, right on top of my kidney, looking for reasons that I kept peeing blood. After about ten minutes, he switched to the other kidney. Same pressure, only this time, ten minutes went by, then thirty, then an hour. The pain was excruciating. I could feel myself getting bruised and sore at having constant pressure on a single spot on my body for hours.

"What's wrong?" I finally asked, sweating from the pain.

"I'm not sure if I see a mass or not."

"Can you please be sure?" I tried to say as nicely as possible to the man turning my kidney into mush.

"Of course! Let's get back to it."

*Of course, because this is a team effort* Another hour went by. The pain was unendurable. I bit my lip to stop screaming, and finally, he stopped.

"I'll send the results to the kidney doctor, and he'll go over them with you." I was shaking from the pain, too tired to protest and demand an answer now. All I wanted was a bed and for all this to be over. They wheeled me into my room. Leila stepped outside to get some lunch. After the transporter left me in my bed, I closed my eyes and just wept.

I felt everything in that moment, the needle pokes, gasping for my next breath, the bruises from the ultrasounds, and every other medical torture that you needed to undergo for the sake of staying alive. Tears ran down my cheeks as my lower lip quivered. It was too much. And that was the moment I did not want to be alive.

*Take me home, Lord. I'm* done! *I'm done with the pain, with the cancer, with all of it. I cannot handle this anymore!* In my spirit I screamed at God. I wept to be done. This struggle finally felt too big for me; this was officially too much for me to handle. *Lord, keep Your word. You wouldn't give us more than we could handle. This is it. It's too much for me. Take me home. Please!*

In my begging God for death, I felt myself drifting, the outside world started fading away, and even my pain was being slowly dulled. And I fell asleep.

"They said the kidney ultrasound took much longer than expected."

"Oh gosh, he's so skinny!"

*I'm not dead?*

"The nurse said it took a lot out of him. It's been a long road…"

*That sounds like Leila? Who's she with?*

Slowly I opened my eyes. Blurry shapes gained focus slowly, and I could see the straight blond of my wife's hair, but I had no idea who the lady in the blue hat was that she was talking to.

"Leila?"

"He's waking up!"

It was already dark out. Same room. I guess no fifth floor today.

"Hi, Bobby!" whispered over the voice, in a long, drawled South Carolina accent.

*That voice! I know that voice. I've fought with that voice!*

"JOYCE?" I caught myself screaming. Suddenly, the fuzzy edges showed my sister's face. She was crying, and on her head was a blue baseball cap with the words TEAM BOBBY emblazoned in orange.

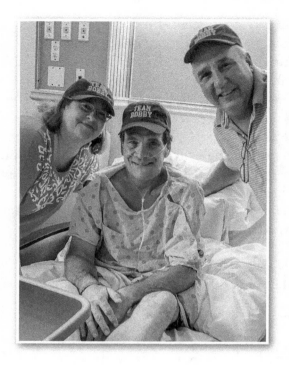

"Surprise!"

I looked around the room, and Leila, Alicia, Joyce and her husband, Tony, and even Mauricio were all wearing the same blue caps. Carefully she sat on the edge of the bed, careful not to break me, and hugged me as tight as she dared. Her tears dripping on my face, and my own tears blubbering down my cheeks. We held each other as we wept. Seeing her made the cancer more real, if that were possible; who she was hugging now was barely a shell of the brother she grew up with. But the opposite was also true for me; she was a reminder that I was not always this walking cadaver riddled with cancer. The pain made me often think that this reality was all I ever was. Our childhood in South Carolina, picking blackberries and surfing, wasn't an illusion. She was proof that I lived.

"What are you doing here?" I asked, grabbing her tightly, making sure I wasn't dreaming this.

"When you told us not to come, I got worried, and we've been coordinating with Leila to make sure you wouldn't find out and not see us."

"I'm so happy you're here, Joyce!

We talked for a long time. Alicia and Mauricio went home, and Leila had a bite to eat on the chair next to me while we caught up. Around 8:00 p.m., the kidney doctor showed up, and we were all reminded of the gravity of the situation.

"Robert, the kidney ultrasound was inconclusive. The technician thought he saw a mass on your left kidney, but I don't see it that way. I'm going to adjust your fluids and keep you here overnight to monitor you. If the urine clears up, we'll send you up to the fifth floor tomorrow."

"And chemo?" asked Leila. "When will that be?"

"Dr. Kaywin will schedule it when you get up there. Try to get some rest." He smiled, making his way out the door.

Leila went home to shower. I stayed talking with Joyce and Tony until they left for their hotel. A few minutes after they said their goodbyes, Leila walked in the door, hair wet, but with a different expression on her face. Sitting on a hospital bed with cancer, you get two kinds of people come see you, friends and family members who look at you with death on their faces, and doctors and nurses who are trained not to show it. The first group is saying their goodbyes before they even know it; the second know better than to get attached.

Right now, Leila was a third kind. She was smiling, and I saw life in her face. For the first time since this process started, she looked at peace, with hope for the future.

"You're not dying!" she said.

"That's good to hear," I said, trying to pass a smile on my face.

"No, you don't get it. I was in the shower, praying, and God spoke to me. He told me you're not dying! He'll take care of the rest." She sat on the bed and held me. We both wept together. It was the end of an overwhelming day, and there was my sign. God sent me a sign through my wife. He had not forgotten me.

She fell asleep in the recliner around midnight, but I still was wide-awake, having slept most of the afternoon after the ultrasound. *My Father, I am in Your hands. Whatever You choose for my life, I am yours. I depend on You for my next breath.* Throughout the night, I took little naps here and there between nurse visits. Some were monitoring my kidney; others were bringing the routine medication or checking for signs of infection.

By the morning, Dr. Kaywin came in alone. "Good news! You're going up today," he said while looking at the notes on my chart made throughout the night. "Once they take you to the fifth floor, we're going to schedule your chemo for the following day. Since it's the oncology floor, the nurses there will monitor you for anything that will prevent you getting chemo, but I'm cautiously optimistic that we're ready."

All that day, we didn't know when they would come and take us up, so no one wanted to go anywhere. Leila packed my bags and left them by the door, ready to go whenever they showed up to take me. By noon, a transporter came and took us up. The rooms on the fifth floor had already been remodeled within the last year or two; the decor was much more modern than that of the fourth floor.

"It looks like a hotel!" said Mauricio, carrying one of the duffel bags full of clothes Leila and I had been accumulating since moving into the hospital.

"Twice as big as the other room!" chimed Alicia, looking around.

More than just in the scenery, something *felt* different in the spirit, like we were over a huge hurdle. But still, I liked Kaywin's words.

*Cautiously optimistic.*

The rest of that day, we waited. The nurses were monitoring my kidneys, heartbeat, temperature, and any other sign that something would go wrong. Leila's watchful eye scrutinized every possibility that chemo would slip through our fingers, and the cancer would be forced to fight another day.

Joyce and her husband, Tony, passed by in the afternoon; they would leave tomorrow, so they spent the afternoon by my side, right through lunch and orange juice and honey-thick waters. It felt unreal. This was *the* day; since I was first diagnosed, I'd been expecting this day. So many delays and moments put off, and if it all went well, God willing, we could see a step forward.

*Let's hope you're around by January,* said a small voice in my head, repeating Kaywin's words, trying to rekindle fear in my head.

*I'll be around.*

In the evening, my son, Robbie, walked in the room. He was able to get off work to see my first chemo. He sat in the recliner and told me about his job, the Dolphins, and his dogs to get my mind off the chemo for a while. By the fourth nurse checkup, all things normal, they finally scheduled the chemotherapy. And Leila was ready to party. "It'll take a few hours for the pharmacy to create the mixtures, and then we'll bring it up when it's ready."

That night, when Alicia and Mauricio showed up, Leila and I were ready. Two nurses were putting on yellow gowns over their scrubs and masks to protect themselves from any accidental chemo spills. While waiting for the medications to arrive, one of the nurses was reading off a checklist.

"You will receive three types of infusion therapies tonight," she said. "Chemotherapy, which will last for ninety minutes. Then you will have a thirty-minute break. Then Keytruda, which will run for forty-five minutes. Another thirty-minute break, and carboplatin as a final infusion, which will run for thirty minutes."

They scanned my bracelet into the computer and then scanned the bags of medication to ensure that the right patient was getting the right medication. One of the nurses hung the first bag of yellow chemicals, while another lifted my sheets to get access to the port in my leg. "You know, you're the first patient I've ever seen that has their port in their leg!" said the brunette nurse with green eyes excitedly. "And I've been here eleven years doing this!"

*Cool.*

"Now I'm going to flush your port with saline, and we'll start with the first chemo."

"Okay." I nodded.

Leila took a seat by my right side and held my hand. Alicia sat on the bed and held my left. Before laying my head on the pillow, I could see Mauricio standing at my feet, watching the whole scene.

"We're not out of the woods yet, Mr. Robert," said the short blond nurse, who couldn't have been any older than Alicia. "By hospital protocol, I have to wait fifteen minutes with you after we start the infusion to make sure you don't have any reactions to the medication."

"What kind of reactions are we looking for?" I asked, not sure I wanted to hear the answer.

"Anaphylactic shock, convulsions, hives, which can lead to death if we don't catch it quick enough."

*That's reassuring.*

"I'll keep time for you, Dad," said Robbie, taking a seat by the window.

I took a deep breath and closed my eyes. My life is in God's hands. I've begged Him to take me home, and here I still am, so if He hasn't taken me yet, He will also see me through this. I grabbed my wife's and my daughter's hands and held them tightly. It was going to be a long night.

"Lord, I am completely in Your hands. You Word says that 'though I walk through the shadow of death, I will fear no evil.' If I die tonight, I go with You, but in any case, I will glorify You with every breath You give me."

Leila started reading out loud the Joyce Meyer healing scriptures. I squeeze my wife's hand and held tight.

"Okay. I'm ready."

# It's Okay, I Got a Bumper!

*Alicia*

"Now, when you're taking the test and you think the questions are getting harder and you think you're going to fail, that's the Devil talkin' to you!" said the blond instructor with the heavy Southern accent in the training video.

*Seriously?*

Orange clouds rolled back, and deep-purple streaks followed the sunset. Light from my laptop illuminated the pile of nursing books, study guides, class notes, and medical scribbles that covered every inch of my desk. I had been at this for weeks now, trying to cram as much information as possible to prepare for the nursing board exam, which, by all accounts, was harder than childbirth.

Most people taking this exam spend the better part of six months studying for it. With my dad in the hospital and all his needs at home, I've barely had a month to study, if *that*. The doctors sent him home a few days ago, monitoring for reactions after his first chemo. No reactions. That was a miracle, and we breathed a sigh of relief when we brought him home.

"Baby! Dinner!" came Maury's voice from the kitchen. He had been cooking for us every night since we came back from the hospital. Which was a godsend, because my mom's idea of cooking is frozen lasagna, and there's only so much Chinese food one can have delivered in a week.

I closed the training video. "Coming!" But behind it was another screen with the practice test I started an hour ago. *Just a few more questions.*

The smell of caramelized onions wafted under the door. Sweet onions mixed with browning butter made my stomach rumble and made it even harder to concentrate.

"ALICIA! DINNER!" came my mom's voice from the dinner table.

"I'M COMING!" I yelled back. A few more questions and I could see how ready I was for the test. If I didn't pass this test, I couldn't become a nurse; maybe I could become a teacher like my mom? After I answered a few more, the screen changed, and the test closed, showing the score.

*Dang.*

"ALICIAAAAA!" came Spapi's voice, gravelly and wheezy. "YOU NEED TO GIVE ME THE SHOT AFTER DINNER!"

*Maybe it's not too late to be a teacher?*

He sat on his recliner after dinner, hanging his gray cane on the wall, and lifted his shirt. There was no fat on his stomach, only saggy skin rippling below his belly button.

"This shouldn't hurt," I said, hoping that was true, slowly pushing the needle into the fat of his belly and emptying the blood thinner. He grimaced and pretended it didn't hurt. I knew better.

"It burns a little." He smiled, rubbing the skin around the injection.

"Don't rub it, Spapi! You'll get a huge bruise!"

"But it burns!"

"Blow on it. It'll make you feel better."

"ARRRRGHH!" he yelled, trying to blow on his belly and sending spittle down his chest.

"Leila?" he turned to my mom and lifted his shirt. He stifled a laugh.

"Not now, honey," she said, turning the page on her book.

*Oh god, I need a shower.*

I lost myself in the marble veining of the tiles as steam filled the shower and the hot water melted the tension on my shoulders. Here, at least I was alone with my thoughts; outside this door the nursing exam couldn't get me. Neither could my dad's constant nagging. It was just the water and me.

*At least he got back his sense of humor.*

Ever since going to the hospital, and since the diagnosis, he'd been a jerk. Snapping at all of us when he felt uncomfortable. He also got this annoying habit of calling Maury for no reason; he would yell, "MAURICIOOOOO!" from his recliner, and Maury would come out of my brother's old room, ask what he needed, and he would just reply, "Nothing."

*Just leave the guy alone! Keep pushing him like that and he's going to leave!*

My mom said Maury was his security blanket. Like the napkins in the hospital. Something he could depend on.

That got me so angry. I started scrubbing my shoulders harder with the loofah.

*Why did he have to smoke? He promised he wouldn't! Now my mom and I are stuck in this situation, and nobody asked for it!* The bubbles were piling up and almost reached my nose. Still, the aggressive scrubbing felt good. I didn't feel the tears running down my face, but the stinging in my eyes wasn't from soap.

*And why is my dad dying of cancer when my father, the man who made my childhood hell and cheated on my mom, gets to live his best life? What kind of God allows for that?*

The scrubbing stopped. The tears did not. Finally, I found the reason I was feeling numb and snapping at everybody. I thought it was the board exam, but no, I was angry with God. It wasn't fair that the man who loved me, even though I wasn't his daughter, was dying in front of my eyes. It wasn't fair that the father who mentally abused my brother and me, who didn't care for God, or being a decent human being for that matter, lived in his big house, happy, not caring for the years of damage he'd done to my family and me.

"What kind of God sees this picture and says, 'I'm okay with this'?" I muttered under my breath. There was a certain relief in knowing whom to be angry at.

For the rest of the week, I stayed in my room, studying for the board exam. Every practice test, and every answered question, buried a little deeper the fear that if I failed, I would have to pay back my scholarship, all sixty thousand dollars of it, and start my life from scratch. On to the next question.

In the mornings, before leaving for work, Maury hugged me from behind. I could feel his enormous arms wrapped tight around my chest, and the prickly kisses of his beard on my cheek as he said goodbye. My dad would send him on errands to the jobsites to keep the work going. He would leave in the mornings, get progress reports from the supervisors, and bring news back to my dad. When news were good, my dad would just clear his throat and stay quiet, staring back at the TV. When news was bad, he would get on the phone and scream at everybody at the top of his lungs to do better.

"EDDIEEEE! DON'T THINK, JUST LISTEN!" He had yelled that this week every day. Something big must be going on at work, and I knew it killed him to be stuck at home and not there, working with his guys.

But today was different! Today was Maury's birthday, so I had a date night planned! After he came back from work, we were going out to an Italian restaurant and forgetting all about the cancer and work and screaming dads. I could hardly contain my excitement as I rifled through the pharmacy textbook. Blah blah blah…OxyContin…fentanyl…diphenhydramine. *Yawn!*

*Date night! We need this! Oh god, I need this.*

That evening, I straightened out my hair, put on my long maxi dress, the one that made my legs look amazing, and the wedges to match. Never mind that I changed my outfit three times or that I finally put on mascara. I looked good!

"You need lipstick!" said my mom from the door. "Go get one from my bathroom."

*Leave it to her to find a flaw!*

"I love you, and you know I'm right." She smiled.

I rolled my eyes.

*Of course she's right!*

He came out of my brother's room ready to go a few minutes later. Blue dress shirt, blue jacket, and a neatly trimmed beard. And whatever cologne was that smelled like sandalwood and balsam.

*Dang!*

"Looking good, birthday boy!" said my mom, giving him a hug. Her small frame looked lost in his arms. This must be what I looked like hugging him too. Even my dad came out to tell us goodbye. Leaning over his cane, he kissed my cheek. When Maury turned to hug him, he turned aside, looking like he was about to throw up.

"Spapi! You okay?"

"Don't get too close to me, Mauricio. With the chemo, I'm like a pregnant woman—I could smell you from your bedroom!"

Maury backed away toward the door. There it was, I thought; cancer showed its presence today. No matter. Today was date night! We were halfway to the door when I heard, "ALICIA! YOU FORGOT TO GIVE ME MY SHOT!"

*There is no end to this!* I sighed.

I ran to the kitchen and pulled the syringe with the blood thinner.

"Sit on the couch, Spapi," I said dryly.

"Ow!" He winced. And part of me felt good about it.

"Okay, now get out of here!" said my mom, rushing us out the door. "Don't call, don't worry about anything, just have fun tonight! Love you!"

*Love you too.*

In the dim, warm bistro lights, modernist abstract paintings faded into the background. With their bold, aggressive brushstrokes and neutral grays and blacks, they were interesting enough to catch the eye without overwhelming the ambience. Over sharp Chianti and a shared appetizer of short ribs, I was able to finally talk with my boyfriend, who more and more felt monopolized by my dad.

"I just don't get it, babe. When will all this be over?"

"When it ends," he said, concealing half a smile.

I looked at him with the least amusement my face could show. Here I was, trying to pour my heart out, and he was making jokes!

*Jackass!*

He swished the wine in his glass and tasted it.

"Take a look at this situation for what it is. He's not dead. We haven't lost yet. A few months ago, we were fighting for him to get his first chemo. Now he has it and there's been no bad reactions."

I took a sip of wine; the acidity in the wine made my mouth pucker.

"This thing is bigger than all of us, and without God to hold us up, we're going down. But I know that His hand is on this. It's probably the easiest thing to say and the hardest thing to do, but trust in His promise. God promised that 'by His wounds we are healed,' and it's in these moments where the trial is that faith counts."

I nodded, saying nothing. I was still angry with God and did not want to spoil the mood, taking some more wine to keep my mouth busy.

"I mean, don't you think it's weird that you and I went on our first date and said 'I love you' for the first time in the same week? By any account, we didn't move fast—we moved at warp speed! Or don't you think it's weird that six weeks after starting to date, I moved into your house? That had to be God!"

"Yeah, that was weird. I still can't believe that happened." I laughed. "I can't believe my parents opened up to you so much and so fast."

The waiter cleared our appetizer and brought two plates of risotto. Aromas of saffron and Parmesan filled the table and explained the growling in my stomach.

"It had to be God!" he said between mouthfuls. "I've never been in any relationship where we've moved so fast and where I've never been more convinced that it's right. Where, by conventional wisdom, it shouldn't have worked. But here we are!"

I felt my cheeks turn warm and hurt from smiling so much.

"Dang, this risotto is good!" Taking another mouthful.

We walked hand in hand to the front door of my house. The solid oak door creaked in its hinges, showing my mom in yoga pants, sneakers, and a T-shirt, my dad behind her, getting ready to leave. Her eyes met mine. Something was wrong.

"He has a fever of 102," she said dryly. "The doctor said that if his temp is over 101, we should go to the hospital. So we're going to the hospital."

*Here we go again!*

It took two minutes for Maury and me to get changed, the glamour of the evening giving way to flip-flops and yoga pants and a ratty T-shirt. This was a painfully constant reminder that cancer was always present and it didn't give up. Whatever happiness this evening gave us was sobered up by this midnight trip to the hospital.

The emergency room already knew his condition from his records; it saved time having him in the system. A nurse trained in oncology patients took us into a private room to wait for the doctor. In the room, the nurse gave him an oxygen mask to help him breathe. Maury asked the nurse why the private room, when last time we had to wait outside.

"Because of the chemotherapy, he is immunocompromised, which means his body can't fight any infections," she told Maury when he asked why we were being moved. She took Spapi's temperature and vitals. "His body already has a fever," she continued, "so he already has an infection. If he stayed with the general population, he could catch whatever they came in with, and it would run rampant through his system."

My mom and I sat on a bench, waiting for the doctor. Spapi was in his wheelchair since he got to the hospital, and Maury was standing by the door, using Spapi's cane for support. None of us wanted to be here.

"Sorry, everybody," came Spapi's hoarse, tired, voice, muffled under the mask.

No one spoke. We were emotionally numb, preparing ourselves for whatever the doctors would tell us next. Eventually, a doctor came in and admitted him. They would monitor him throughout the night and alert Dr. Kaywin in the morning for him to decide how to proceed.

"Just waiting for a bed to become available. Hang tight," he said before leaving.

We knew the drill. Seeing my face, Maury sat next to me on the bench while my mom had gone to use the bathroom. I didn't realize how cold I was until the warmth of his arm thawed mine.

"I'm sorry, babe," I started, not knowing what to say to make this situation better. Who could have told me that our date night would end in the hospital with my parents? Was this really the life he wanted? How was he not running for the hills?

He started laughing.

"I was just thinking, we had date night, on my birthday, and it ended in the ER, with none of the usual pleasures. I feel cheated!"

*My dad was right in front of us!*

I smacked him on the shoulder. Hard. Which made him laugh harder, which made me laugh too. And suddenly it wasn't so bad. His dumb joke broke through the fog of emotions, and it made the night go a little easier.

Around five in the morning, he got a room, and my mom made us go home and get some rest. She stayed with him and would call us in the morning with news. I don't remember how we fell into my bed that night; I just remember Maury's arm around mine, and that was enough.

In the morning, we walked into his hospital room on the third floor. The tower building was one of the oldest parts of the hospital, and their rooms were barely larger than my parents' walk-in closet. Immediately after we opened the door, his bed was to our right, and between his bed and the wall was a chair for a single visitor; anyone else had to stand. My mom was sitting on the chair next to the bed. It was clear she had slept there, from the rustled blanket and pillow that still covered part of the armrest. Spapi was distracted on his phone when we came in.

"What do we know?" asked Maury, taking in a deep breath, bracing himself.

"So far, he has an infection. Blood work came back a few minutes before you guys showed up, and it shows his hemoglobin is below 8," she said, putting down the hospital binder with all the cancer notes, Spapi's medication lists, and doctor's orders since he was diagnosed.

"That's bad. And it explains why he's so tired lately."

"What do you mean?" asked Maury.

"Hemoglobin carries oxygen through the blood. The less hemoglobin, the less oxygen gets to the body and makes you feel tired. Because of chemo, red blood cells die, and your hemoglobin goes down."

*Thank God for nursing school!*

"Normal hemoglobin for him should be between 14 and 18."

"What happens if it gets lower than 8?" Spapi interrupted. His phone was on his lap, and he had been listening to the conversation.

I hesitated to say it. We were already in the hospital, he already had cancer, and I didn't want to say anything else that could add more fear to this situation.

"Well?"

"Your organs could start shutting down."

He stayed silent. The hospital staff hadn't even brought breakfast to his room yet, and fear was already in the room. He closed his eyes and stayed silent for a few seconds. None of us knew what to do.

"Okay, then." He finally spoke, going back to his phone.

"But that won't happen, Spapi!" I said quickly, trying to reassure him. "They'll give you a blood transfusion before it gets to that."

"I know. God already told your mom I'm not dying."

*Huh?*

"Leila, tell them the story!"

Seeing the puzzled look on our faces amused him. Knowing my dad, this wasn't the first time he had her tell this story. And by the eagerness in his voice, he would listen to it over and over as long as my mom's patience allowed it. I sat at the edge of the bed and faced my mom.

She sat up on the recliner, closed her eyes, and drew a careful smile on her face. She paused a few times before speaking, as if the words she was about to tell would fall apart and shatter like glass unless she spoke them very carefully and took her time. No one made a sound.

"You don't know this, Coosie, but the last time he was in the hospital, when you guys would come to spend time with him and I went home to shower, I would cry my eyes out. Twenty-three hours a day I felt I had to be strong in front of you, but that hour when I showered was my moment of breaking down. Every night I would cry and pray the Our Father, because that was the only prayer I knew. I would say it over and over and over and over."

She took a pause. Trying to remember every detail. I remembered to breathe then.

"One night, I was praying, and God spoke to me. Not in an audible voice, but a voice that would shake your spirit down to its core. A voice that felt more real than you—that is, strong and good rolled into one—and that knew me."

*Say it!*

"'He's not dying. He is not going to die. Just trust in Me. Everything will be okay.'"

"I cried so much harder. It felt like everything that was holding me together gave way. But when it was over, I felt such a peace. And that hasn't gone away." She smiled.

Already, tears were running down my face. Maury was standing on the corner, looking at my parents. I felt goose bumps, and more tears. From behind me I could hear sounds like a vacuum cleaner with something stuck in it coming from my dad's throat. His eyes glittered with tears, and he was trying not to cry, listening to the story. Trying to keep it together.

He smacked the mattress with his hand.

"God is so good!"

"Spapi! There's an IV in your arm!"

"I don't care! I'm going to live!"

That afternoon, a nurse brought the update from Dr. Kaywin. Spapi needed to stay in the hospital until the infec-

GOD HAS THE FINAL WORD

tion cleared. They started him on a course of antibiotics and fluids to replace nutrients lost from the chemo. When the infection cleared, then they would order a blood transfusion, which would offset the effects of the next chemo.

*Smart.*

Over the next few days, I would stay home to study until the evenings. There was still a mountain of material to cover, but if I kept the pace, I just might cover everything before the board exam. Maury would leave in the mornings to check on the jobsites and run back and forth to the hospital with papers for my dad to sign, send e-mails, etc. My mom stayed with my dad most of the day, until we went over in the evenings and she had an hour to herself at home.

That Friday, Spapi's infection was finally clearing up. By Sunday, the antibiotics had run their course, and the scans taken during his hospital stay showed the cancer was not growing anymore. He wasn't healed yet, but it was a step in the right direction. My mom's words from God gave me hope too. Could we actually see an end to this cancer that had a happy ending? It felt too fragile just yet. And before that hope had a chance to set, fear showed up too.

*What if it's fake? What if my mom's grief is playing a trick on her?*

I was suspicious of trusting in God; after all, He was the one that let my dad get cancer while my biological father could cheat his way through the world and get away with it. I couldn't get over that. One day, God and I would have to talk about this, but for now, I closed my books for the day.

That evening, while my mom was home, Spapi was sitting up on the bed, eating little bites of mashed potatoes and chicken from the side of his mouth. The ball of cancer in his jaw was still the same size, disfiguring his already-sunken face.

"Spapi, how much do you weigh now?" Maury asked, taking a seat in a folding chair a nurse had brought in and forgot.

"Ah, 149," he said between mouthfuls, not looking up from his plate.

"So you've lost even more weight since you've been here?"

"I was 153 last week, so…yeah?"

It would have been funny if it weren't so frustrating. In this week alone, we'd heard from doctors that the cancer wasn't advancing, yet he was not getting better. I heard from my mom that he was eating more, but he still lost weight! One step forward, two steps back, and two more forward, and we were still in the same dang place!

"Spapi, how can you be so relaxed at this whole thing?" I asked, looking into his pallid, greenish face. "How are you not screaming angrily at God that you're in this bed right now?"

He put down his plastic fork on the plate, and his piercing blue eyes met mine.

"Alicia, God didn't do this to me. I did this to myself! God is merciful enough to love me through this!" He took a sip of water from the cup on his tray. "You know the kind of life I've lived. I tried to raise you kids knowing about God, but I also walked away from Him. I've smoked countless packs of cigarettes a day, I've smoked pot, drank, you name it. I put myself on this bed. And if I die, I die! And I will praise God with my last breath, like I promised Him the day I got diagnosed. And if I get out of this bed, it's because He's getting me out of it. But I will not, for one second, blame God for this situation."

We stayed quiet for a while. It was getting difficult for him to catch his breath.

"So on top of being a dang redneck, you're also a dang stoner! You're a mess, man!" said Maury from the corner, looking at Dad to see how he'd react.

"Babe!"

"Look who's talking! Dang foreigner!" came his reply.

"SPAPI!"

They both started laughing at each other.

*They're both the same!*

"Can you believe it, man? Here I am, a stoner redneck in Miami, with cancer, being 'nursemaided' by this dang foreigner."

"Listen here, old man!" said Maury, sitting up at the edge of his seat. This was going to get good! "I was born in Cuba, you were born in South Carolina, in Miami, so we're *both* foreigners!"

Spapi was laughing and slapping his thigh until his eyes got watery. We spent the rest of the evening listening to classic Southern rock and hearing Spapi singing the Acapulco Gold jingle.

"No stems, no seeds!"

"Where's that from?" asked Maury.

"You've never seen Cheech and Chong?"

"Not really."

"Dang foreigner!" he said, shaking his head.

By next morning, a nurse was reading to him a consent paper for the blood transfusion.

"You may experience any of the following side effects commonly associated with receiving a blood transfusion: fever, chills, skin rashes, shortness of breath, acute pulmonary edema, shock, and in extremely rare cases, death. If you understand these risks as I have explained them to you, please sign here," she said, holding up the paper on the clipboard.

"Err...okay," said Spapi, signing, eyes wide and a nervous smile on his face. "Then I can go home?"

"After you're done with the transfusion, I can start getting your discharge papers ready. But you're getting two units of blood. It's going to take a while."

After she left, he turned to Mauricio. "At this point, everything that may make you better also has a chance to kill you. You're literally gambling with your life."

It was close to an hour before the nurse came with the blood. Spapi, already aggravated, was taking it out on us, nagging my mom to talk to another nurse to get his discharge papers processed to save time. He had a radiation appointment that same afternoon.

Seeing the frustration in my mom's face, the nurse hung the blood bag on the dispenser and attached the tube to the machine that would pump it into his veins. "It doesn't work that way. I have to first monitor you for fifteen minutes to make sure there are no reactions. Then it takes anywhere from two to three hours for the first bag to be done. Then we have another bag to get and do this process all over again."

"You *gotta* be kidding me!"

"Wish I were, Mr. Germroth. But you'll see how quickly you feel better after this is over. Just sit back and relax."

We stayed quiet while the nurse was looking at my dad, then the clock, and back to my dad.

"You're in the clear," she said. "I'll be back after the first bag is done to monitor your progress." She left quickly after. Already my dad was famous in the hospital for being a difficult patient; once he got something in his head, good luck getting him to change his mind.

*Normal nurses are heroes. His nurses were saints.*

By early afternoon, they had finished the second bag. No reactions, no edema, no death! After enough nagging by my dad, the nurse brought his discharge papers, and we walked to Miami Cancer Institute for his radiation appointment.

Leading the radiology department was Dr. Mehta, a deeply refined, dark-skinned man with a congenial laugh, who explained the procedure again to my parents while Maury and I were standing toward the back of the examination room.

"We're targeting the spots in your jaw and your brain today. First, we'll start with your jaw and irradiate the spots that prevent you from eating normally. You'll feel some itching around the area, and you'll feel your teeth and jawbone move in there. It's normal."

"What about the numbness on part of my lower lip?" he asked.

"I'm afraid that's dead nerve. We don't expect you to regain sensation there."

"We'll take what we can get," said my mom, grabbing on to his hand. "Better a numb lower lip than a golf ball in your jaw made of cancer."

The men nodded in agreement.

"Now, onto the brain! Dr. Kaywin has assembled a team of doctors from all over the world that will be working on the two spots in your brain. We're going to use a machine called the CyberKnife, which can kill individual cells in your brain while leaving healthy tissue unaffected. This is bleeding-edge stuff! I think you're the first person in the States to get this procedure."

After the meeting, two assistants took my dad to the prep room, and they would get him ready. "You guys go home. You need to study," my mom told us. "I'll stay with him and keep you posted."

We ordered Chinese that night. It was the first time since he went to the hospital that we were all eating together as a family. Plastic to-go boxes lined the kitchen table: fried rice, egg rolls, and honey garlic chicken were being passed around as Spapi told us about the radiation.

"They said I'd be feeling the fatigue and dizziness tomorrow and the next day," he said, spooning clear seafood soup onto his lips.

"Robert, don't do that!" interrupted my mom. "Start at the beginning!"

He took a long pause, in part to swallow his soup, then to gather his thoughts.

"Okay. From where y'all left me, they wheeled me into another room that had all these doctors working around a table where patients lay down. Right in front of the table was a mechanical arm that could swivel all along the table, to apply radiation to any part of the body."

He took another spoonful of soup. Another long pause.

"The doctors pressed a button and turned the table into a reclining chair so they could sit me upright. Then, they put this brace around my neck and spent most of the time adjusting the brace so I could not move, and they could get exact alignment with the laser."

"Radiosurgery," I interrupted.

"The laser," he insisted. "On another screen that showed my latest scans, they checked and double-checked their measurements. That was when my nose started itching. Just when I couldn't move a millimeter! They started with my brain. I half-expected to smell bacon, thinking the laser would burn. But it just showed a bright light and that was it. The mechanical arm changed angle and zapped another part of my head."

"And your hip?" asked Maury, biting halfway into a spring roll.

"Same thing. They laid me down on my side, adjusted the arm, and zapped there too," he said without looking up from his soup. "Alicia," he continued, "after dinner, you need to give me the blood thinner shot again. The nurses took care of that in the hospital, but I need you now."

"Dr. Kaywin didn't change your medication? He didn't suggest an oral blood thinner?" I asked, hoping for little more freedom.

"No. He says down the line he will but for now to stay on the injection, that it has better results and helps with the pain in my chest."

"Is that still a thing?" asked Maury.

"Yeah, he still has cancer wrapping around a major blood vessel. The blood thinner helps to ease that pain by making blood flow through there better," I answered. "Spapi, Dr. Kaywin will probably put you on an oral blood thinner if cancer starts dying in that area. When is your next chemo?"

"Day after tomorrow."

The infusion wing at Miami Cancer Institute felt more like an expensive spa than a hospital where people were fighting for their lives. Ornate, oversize light fixtures and floor-to-ceiling windows flooded with natural light. Each room held two recliners, with built-in TV sets and frosted glass privacy partitions, where patients could change and be comfortable without feeling alienated. We drove with plenty of time to spare for his appointment, sitting in the waiting area until a nurse in turquoise scrubs called for Robert. Spapi insisted on getting it done as early as possible, in case anything went wrong, like the pharmacy sending the wrong medication, or if the doctors forgot to send a paper to the insurance, then they would have time to fix it. Thank God nothing happened, and like clockwork, our nurse, Barbara, walked us to his room. After taking his temperature, confirming his age, name, and birthdate, she scanned his medical bracelet and phoned the pharmacy for the medication.

Barbara patted my dad's chest, looking for the port. That was when my dad, who was wearing basketball pants with the tear-away snaps, pulled them apart, and showed her the port on his leg.

"Oh my goodness!" yelled Barbara excitedly. "You're the second person I've ever seen that has the port on their leg! This is so exciting!"

"Nurses get excited about the weirdest things!" said Maury

*But I know exactly how she felt!*

After an hour, the pharmacy sent the medications. He would get three infusions: chemotherapy, carboplatin, and Keytruda.

We sat around him as the first medication slowly traveled down the tube into the port in his leg. My mom held his hand. Maury and I stood by the door in case he needed anything. He turned on the TV on his recliner and watched football replays. It felt surreal. The last time he had chemo, we were all ready to say our farewells, thinking death was in the room with us. This time, he grumbled over how well the Patriots were doing this season.

"Leila," said Spapi, finally turning off the TV in frustration, "read to me." From her oversize purse she pulled out Joyce Meyer's book on spiritual healing.

"Let's go get a table so you can study a while," said Maury, wanting to give them privacy. "I need to get some work done, too, and they're not going anywhere for a few hours." My mom's voice faded as we walked down the hall. ""For I will restore health to you and heal you of your wounds,' says the Lord.'"

*Amen.*

I struggled to understand my parents' faith, their willingness to trust a God they never saw, and in the face of a crippling death sentence, they remained steadfast. Every new piece of bad news, they did not get discouraged, but instead they would leave it in God's hands. "He is healed, even if we can't see it now." They would say it was not up to us to figure it out, just to believe. Nursing school didn't teach this part of the cancer process, the belief that on the other side of it there could be a happy ending. I didn't dare to let myself imagine it. Things were bad now; how much worse could they be if I allowed myself to hope and he ended up dying anyway? My nails dug into my palm, leaving red imprints from the tension as I walked. We sat in the lounge area, grabbing a table by the window overlooking the hospital grounds.

"You know he's going to be okay, right?" said Maury.

"Huh? Yeah, I know. Hope is the last thing you lose, right?"

*Especially if you don't have it.*

That night, from the shower I could see the whole bathroom filling with steam as the hot water made my skin itch. Here I felt most at peace, where the world was locked out. No matter what happened outside, in here at least it was quiet, with only the constant run of the water and the itching, soothing heat.

*He won't die. Just trust in Me.*

I knew that voice. It was the same voice my mom felt. Now I knew it wasn't fake, and now I realized it wasn't her grief lying to her, or any other delusion. This was a voice that made all my hairs stand on end, and it felt like He knew me. He spoke to me like He knew the deepest part of me. The voice was warm, strong, and comforting, and completely opposite to the hurt and anger and helplessness that I had come to feel every day. This voice did not know limits, and hearing it, you knew that there was nothing it couldn't do. My shoulders started shaking, and I held myself, under the running water, as the tears came.

A lot happens at once when you hear the voice of God. I remember feeling relief, the assurance that the voice was speaking the truth, a deep truth that wasn't based on our reality, but rather, reality bows to Him. And almost immediately, I remember feeling guilty for being angry with Him. It made me feel like I had been angry at the good guy all along, and He didn't blame me for it! There was nothing but waves of love in that moment, love that knew what I was feeling, and it didn't stop Him from loving me. Which felt worse. I couldn't hold on to my anger anymore, no matter how hard I tried. I couldn't allow myself to not feel anymore, to keep hope locked in to protect myself from an unavoidable tragedy. *Your will be done.*

*Okay, I trust You,* came the words in my spirit. *Whatever happens now, I trust You.*

Over the next few days, I felt light, and tingly, like a scab had been peeled off my spirit. I went to work, studied, but the usual fears with my dad, and with the test, were dulled, as if they were happening to somebody else and not me. I walked around in a bubble, and nothing bad was getting through. I only felt His voice and the imprint it left. Eventually, that feeling faded, but the anger and resentment never returned.

A few weeks later, toward the end of July, it was finally time for the board exam. The months I spent studying in hospital chairs, at my desk, buried beneath textbooks, and talking to my classmates culminated into tomorrow. Tomorrow I would take the test that determined if I became a registered nurse or would have to pay back sixty thousand dollars' worth of scholarship. I don't recall much the night before the test; I only remember being nervous, not eating, and not sleeping. The anxiety was real.

The testing center was an unassuming building an hour away. We were instructed to arrive an hour early to check in. This, I would come to find out, meant being patted down, all personal possessions confiscated until the end of the test, glasses had to be inspected for cheating devices, and they even inspected your hair—to make sure there wasn't anything hidden there that could give you an advantage. There were even special restrictions on going to the bathroom, so test administrators strongly advised to use the bathroom beforehand.

Adrenaline kicked in, and the anticipation felt like moments before a fight in the arena. You were as close to naked as possible and made to fight a monster with only what was in your head. A monster that changed shape on you, depending on how you answered questions. If you answered right, the questions would become harder, to discourage you from feeling confident. If you answered wrong, they would become easier, trying to lure you into a false sense of security. It was a very smart monster.

At 8:00 a.m. sharp, after the final examinee was inspected from head to flip-flops, the administrator marked, "Begin!" First impressions of this test were exactly what I heard from those that passed it. "If I had known how hard the NCLEX actually was, I wouldn't have become a nurse."

*And. They. Were. Spot. On.*

Every question was hard, and every answer looked right. I remembered the blond lady from the training videos: "But which answer was the *most* right?" Great question! I had expected the test to turn off at 75 questions. The test varied from person to person taking into account how many answers were correct or not. In other words, the test decided how long it should be—you were at its mercy for as long as it wanted, up until question 255, but it was very rare for someone to get that many questions.

At question 254, I was paralyzed.

*Lord, You have carried me this far. I trust in You for my future.* I submitted my answer, and the screen turned off. The test was finished. I wouldn't know the results until tomorrow, so this would be another night without sleeping. A sense of numbness set in after I left the classroom. The next thing I remember is opening the door to my house and Maury holding me in his harms as I shook uncontrollably.

That night, Maury had fallen asleep on my bed. I tried to access the system to see if they had posted the scores early. No such luck. I checked every hour. Still no. And every time I checked, I felt a different kind of fear creep in; it wouldn't be so bad if I failed, I thought. But what if I have to go through this again?

*Oh god, no!*

By 9:00 a.m., Maury and I were at the computer. I already received texts from some people that the scores were up! But it wasn't loading on our screen! Maury kept refreshing the website, trying to make the computer work and trying to keep me from going into a nervous breakdown at the same time. Until finally…

"YOU PASSED!" he said, spinning in my office chair, which I was sure would break under his weight.

"Wait, wait! Let me confirm with the board of nursing. They'll show my license status. Maybe it was a mistake!" *Please be active, please be active, please be active!*

"Well?"

"License status: ACTIVE! I passed!" I grabbed his face, and I kissed him over and over! He was still recovering from that when I gave him my phone and said, "Take video and follow me!" We walked to the kitchen, where my dad was sitting on the counter with his head in his arms and my mom was making pancakes for him.

"I passed!"

She immediately dropped the pan on the stove, jumping up and down, hugging me so tight until she fell on the kitchen floor laughing. "YES, YES, YES, YES! YOU PASSED! I'M DONE!" she cried. "She's a grown-up now!"

*Dignity be damned.*

I looked over at Spapi; it was weird he wasn't saying anything.

"What's wrong with him?" I asked my mom as she was getting off the floor.

"We had an early PET scan this morning and just got back. He's pretty drugged up."

Spapi started bumping his head on the palm of his hand repeatedly.

"Spapi, don't do that. You'll hurt yourself!" I said, grabbing his hand and setting it on the table.

He grabbed the Band-Aid and gauze pad on his arm, where the nurses injected the contrast, and taped it to his forehead. "It's okay, Coosie!" he said, slurring his words. "I got a *bumper*!"

His head swayed back and forth until it came down hard on the Formica.

*Thunk!*

# You're Not Dying of Cancer

*Robert*

The waters in Folly Beach in the summer were wild and unforgiving. If you hesitated even for one second, or lost your balance, waves would swallow you up and slam your board down to the craggy rocks below. That was the best part of surfing there, the thrill! Tasting salt and sea-foam as you balanced on a waxed board, hunting for the largest waves, just barely missing the danger below. And once you caught one, you could see the roofs of the beach houses, three stories high, your stomach twisting into knots from the rush. Then the wave would crash, sending cold water everywhere and cooling the sunburn forming on your back.

It was a wild freedom.

The toilet water looked like those waters too, turbulent. I had been staring at it, bowled over and clutching the marble countertop, waiting for the vomit to come. The face staring back at me showed a beaten old man, wrinkled and deformed, with a cancer ball where his chin used to be. And green! A skinny, wrinkled green old man who was waiting to throw up and not getting anywhere.

Ever since chemo started, side effects would show up a few days later. You hear a lot about what side effects you would have: hair loss, shaking in your bones, constant heat, pain, and nausea. At first, it was hard to notice any of them, not because they were too mild to notice, but because I was already in constant pain from the cancer. Then came the nausea, slick and heavy, like tar at the pit of your stomach, coating your mouth with saliva and sending you running from the recliner to the nearest toilet.

And here I was.

"HUUUURRGHHHK!" Dry heaving.

"Just get it together, Robert!" I yelled at the man in the toilet. And then then he yelled back at me.

"HUUUURRGHHK!" More dry heaving.

*I hate these conversations.*

Back in the recliner, I felt the padded cushions envelop me as I gripped the armrest, trying to ride out the nausea and the pain and whatever side effects were coming. I closed my eyes.

"Robert!" yelled Leila from the kitchen as she folded laundry. "Sit up straight! It's noon!"

"Leave me alone, woman!" was all I could muster. "Let me sleep!"

She rolled her eyes and went back to folding. After a while, I felt the outside world, the TV preacher, Leila and her laundry, and the hum of the dryer fade away. Every day after chemo was like that, and the only thing that broke the monotony were the visits to Kaywin's office to see if I was getting better.

"No hair loss, that's good," Kaywin said. His hands were at my throat, gloved fingers palpating my lymph nodes, checking whether I had any tumors there. "And you haven't been throwing up?"

I looked at Leila.

"No," she answered from her seat. "Just lots of dry heaving."

"That's better than expected," he said, now moving his stethoscope to my back. "Take a deep breath for me."

As I was sucking air, Kaywin paused and moved on to the next lung.

"Good. Have you been tired?" he asked, sitting back down on his chair.

"Oh yeah!" I said. "This thing wears you out, man!"

*Finally, someone was paying attention to what I was feeling.*

Leila took a deep breath.

"That's to be expected," said Kaywin, taking his seat in front of us. "See, the chemo kills everything. We give it with the goal that it will kill the cancer before it kills you. But one of the first things to die off are red blood cells, and they carry oxygen to your muscles. So it will be very difficult to move. You'll have no energy."

*Preach it, baby!*

I threw a told-you-so look at Leila.

She returned her own dirty look.

"Because of that," continued Kaywin, making a motion to his assistant to document, "I'm ordering weekly blood tests on you to monitor your weight, hemoglobin, and hematocrit levels. By monitoring these things, we can determine if your hemoglobin falls too low, and we can get you another blood transfusion."

I was already looking forward to being back in the recliner. And now Leila couldn't tell me anything. This was the perfect excuse for her to leave me alone.

"This just means, Robert," continued Kaywin, "that it's that much more important for you to exercise and walk around."

*You're kidding!*

I looked at Leila; she was smiling menacingly, which meant I could kiss goodbye my recliner.

"Why?" I asked, dreading the answer.

"When you exercise and need more oxygen to your muscles, the brain sends a signal to start producing more red blood cells. It won't happen sitting down. You can also help it along by eating foods high in iron, like liver and spinach or kale."

Leila winced at the mention of liver; she hated the flavor. But even that did not stop her from beaming at Kaywin's orders. Right away, I knew I'd never hear the end of it.

Grabbing her purse as we were ready to go, Leila turned to Kaywin. "How's he looking?"

"Well…" Kaywin hesitated. "We still have a long way to go," he said, being careful not to give us false hope. "He was dangling by his fingertips on the edge of a cliff. Now he's standing at the very edge of it. It's a delicate process, but the goal is to walk him back off that cliff."

She didn't hesitate. "But with God, everything is possible!"

Kaywin smiled. "That's the attitude! Don't lose that!"

The next Monday, Mauricio took me to the first business appointment we had in months. Getting dressed that morning, I realized my company polo dangled, bony shoulders poking through it. Even the belt, I had to poke new holes into the leather so my pants wouldn't fall off.

We drove up to a client's house in Coral Gables, where they wanted to renovate their master bathroom. The house inside had been modernized, LED lights, white marble island in the kitchen, and sleek white walls with brushed nickel accents. The bathroom needed to match; you could see the pink Formica countertops and oversize vanity light bulbs that were popular in the nineties. A roman tub, built into the ground, occupied most of the square footage.

"Only new parents use the tub. You guys probably haven't used this since the Clinton administration." They laughed nervously from the doorway, tense that two strangers were in their bathroom, commenting on their house. It was a normal reaction, seen it a million times, but it helped me get settled into the routine.

Mauricio measured the layout while I asked the routine questions. "Will you be relocating the toilet? Will you still want to keep the tub? What about this large window that faces your neighbor's wall?" They looked at each other; neither had a clue. They probably saw on Pinterest what they wanted and didn't consider the behind-the-scenes requirements to make this happen.

I set my notepad on the Formica. "Let me help you guys. You want a bigger shower. Unless you're passing the house down to your kids anytime soon, make yourselves more comfortable with a bigger shower. We can remove the tub and use that drain to move the toilet. That'll save you some money."

They sighed, and their stance relaxed, the wife's arms uncrossed, all signs that they wouldn't fight about the design after we left.

"And the window?" she finally asked.

"Cover it up. With the tub, you were sitting and the wall covered you. Now with a shower, do you really want to give the neighbor a show?" They laughed easily now, making jokes to each other.

"How soon can you get us a price?" asked the husband.

"I'll e-mail you next week. Give your info to Mauricio."

As Mauricio took their information, I leaned against the bathroom counter, trying to catch my breath and hide it from the clients. No one wanted a contractor that could drop dead in the middle of their home renovation. Everything inside me shook, and it felt like my organs were going a thousand miles an hour, clenching and vibrating, with a mind of their own.

Back in the car, Mauricio drove back to my house.

"Forget the other appointments for today. I can't! Let's go home," I said, trying to settle into the car seat. I dreamed about the recliner; all the energy I thought I had was spent.

"I had a feeling this would take a lot out of you. But you did good! It's the first time you got out of the house for work since chemo," he said, keeping his eyes on the road. "You're doing okay. Little by little." He patted my knee. "Let's get you some lunch first."

I said nothing. My chin itched.

On our last visit to the nutritionist, she recommended a liquid diet since my mouth was a mess to eat anything more complex than pancakes. Leila came up with the idea of a smoothie a few months ago, but with everything that happened with the hospital, I forgot about them. Now we were driving down Bird Road, and "Smoothie King" was flashing in the distance.

"Turn here, now! RIGHT NOW!" I pointed to the entrance we were about to miss.

"What?"

I have to give it to Mauricio; he could be driving and I could yell an instruction out of the blue and he didn't miss a beat! In a typical Miami driver move, he jerked the steering wheel, skipping two lanes and turning the car into the shopping center, squealing tires and hitting the curb. Parking just outside of Smoothie King.

"Would you look at that! We made it!"

"Are you crazy? You could have killed us!" yelled Mauricio, eyes wide.

"Don't look at me! You were driving!" I giggled.

He sat quietly for a minute, hand on the steering wheel, trying to figure what just happened. After coming up with nothing, he just shrugged and got out of the car. "You're buying!" he said, holding the door open for me.

We made the line, got to the cashier, and Mauricio ordered first. On a massive wall-to-wall board next to me were all the different smoothies, some for losing weight, some for building muscle, some to caffeinate you while you built muscle and lost weight, and some to make you go to the bathroom. Blenders roared on and off, pulsing and liquefying fruits, powders, milk, and some brown stuff into an even mixture that looked like wet concrete.

"Robert!" I felt a tap on my shoulder. Turning around, I noticed it was Mauricio.

"You didn't hear me call to you? The cashier's been waiting for you for a while. It's your turn."

I still had no idea what to get. So I turned to the cashier, a stocky short kid with glasses whose name tag read "Edwin," for help.

"Listen," I said, leaning closer, making sure he heard me over the noise of the blenders. "I need to put on weight, like, a lot of it. What you got?" He knew the board by heart, top to bottom. Didn't even have to look at it.

"You want the Hulk!" he said, punching the order into the computer before I had a chance to decide.

'Whoa, whoa, whoa! Hold on now!" Trying to stop him. "I ain't done! How many calories does it have?"

"The biggest size," he said, pointing to a chart on the board, "is 1,400 calories."

"I need at least 3,500 a day." Maybe this was a bad idea.

"We can add more stuff to it. See the list at the bottom?" he said, pointing to another dang list I missed.

"How about peanut butter?" suggested Mauricio.

"Yeah! Peanut butter, aaaand butter pecan ice cream!"

"Already comes with it," said Edwin. "But I'm adding the peanut butter."

"You need kale too," chimed in Mauricio. "Dark leafy greens, remember? For the iron."

"Oh yeah, add that too!"

"In!" said Edwin, seemingly unable to speak in anything short of a yell. *Jeez, this guy is caffeinated.*

"Okay, so what have we got so far?"

"We got bananas, we got peanut butter, we got sugar, weight gainer, cocoa, butter pecan ice cream, aaaand kale!"

"Add strawberries too."

"In!"

It took twenty minutes to decide what I wanted, and Edwin had it in my hand in two. Mauricio was halfway done with his smoothie by the time we were back in the car.

"How is it?"

"Not bad! I could do this again." It took me the rest of the afternoon to finish that shake. But it was the first time I didn't have a hard time eating something other than pancakes.

Back at home, there were yellow sticky notes in the fridge, in Leila's handwriting, which wasn't unusual, since she often left reminders there, but I could tell these were meant to stay. She taped them to the fridge to make sure of that.

Mauricio leaned over one of them. "Huh, nice!" he said, sipping the last of his smoothie. Every yellow square had a quote from Scripture with the reference. I'd heard of pastors saying to do that years ago, to surround yourself with the Word. Leila was notorious for everything in its place, so even something out of place on the fridge would drive her nuts. This would have bothered her unless she came up with the idea.

"Huh!" I took another sip of my shake. Reading each to myself.

> *He will make an utter end of it. Affliction will not rise up a second time. (Nah. 1:9)*

> *"For I will restore health to you, and heal you of your wounds" Says the Lord. (Jer. 30:17)*

> *Therefore I say to you, whatever things you ask when you pray, believe that you receive them, and you will have them. (Mark 11:22–24)*

*Okay, God, I'm doing it.*

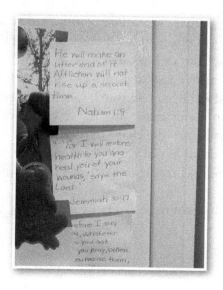

Feeling the ache in my legs and in my back, I went to my recliner and sat down. I put some TV on and fell asleep, drifting to the sound of a preacher on TBN. It was already the evening when I woke up from my nap. The smell of roasted onions and other earthy, grassy odors told me Mauricio was in the kitchen. I heard Leila and Alicia's voice coming from the office. Talking about Mauricio taking a trip in a few days or something.

At eye level to my recliner, right by my head, was a rectangular frame filled with baby photos of the kids. My favorite was a circular one of me holding Robbie, my firstborn, when he was a baby thirty years ago. There was another sticky note over that photo.

*I shall not die, but live, and declare the works of the Lord. (Ps. 118:17)*

I felt the Holy Spirit make me pay attention to that.

"Robert, get up!" yelled Leila coming into the kitchen. "You've been in that chair all day. Come on! Sit at the table!" It took a few minutes to walk the ten steps to my chair at the table from the recliner. I had to hold on to the wall to get enough balance and step into the kitchen floor from our sunken den. I felt Mauricio watch me, steaming pot in hand, ready to drop it and chase after me in case I went down. By the time I made it to the chair, I was out of breath. The three of them set the table and handed out plates for dinner. I was too busy to notice, trying to catch my breath and feeling my organs shaking.

"Babe, I forgot to tell you, my cousin Ana called, asking how you're doing."

"Okay..."

"They want to come and see you. No one from the family has really seen us except your sister in the hospital." I held my head in my hand for support. That took pressure off my back and let me feel at least like some part of me wasn't shaking inside.

"Robert, would you stop holding your head in your hands?"

Everyone stood still. The kids looked at each other, frozen. Alicia still had a fork in her mouth.

"I'm sick of seeing you with your head in your hands! You do it all the time!" she said, returning to her food.

"I didn't realize I was doing it, babe. I'm sorry!"

*Don't fight the angry woman. She can take you now.*

I kissed her cheek slowly and carefully. She softened up and went back to talking with Alicia. Mauricio and I exchanged looks without them noticing.

*Dangerrrr.*

And just as quickly as the yelling came, it passed. She caressed my back and sweetly, looking into my eyes, said, "It just looks like you're feeling bad all the time. And I hate seeing you like that. Do you feel bad now?"

"No," I lied. "I'm okay." Reaching for the glass of ice tea and taking a sip through the straw. She leaned in for a kiss. I felt her lips on half of mine, the right side, where the tumor deformed my chin and was completely numb.

*It's cancer. Of course I feel bad now! I feel bad all the time! There hasn't been a moment since the diagnosis when I don't feel bad or in pain. But if I tell you, you'll feel worse. And that's not going to do us any favors.*

A few days later, at MCI...

"Have you been eating more?" asked the medical assistant at Miami Cancer Institute taking my weight on the scale. I nodded. In my jeans, white company polo, and black socks, I mustered 157 pounds.

"I guess!"

"You've gained six pounds since your last weigh-in at the main hospital. That's so good!"

I smiled while putting on my shoes. Mauricio handed me back my phone, sunglasses, and the medical binder that we took for every appointment. Today we would do blood work and monitor the hemoglobin, meet the nutritionist, and confirm the next chemo.

She took us to another room where a tall bearded nurse in green scrubs was entering my information into the computer. Even sitting, he towered over me.

"Okay, Robert, make a fist for me?" I remembered Alicia saying that when nurses have difficulty finding the vein, they go fishing for it with the needle inside your arm. At the last second, before the needle touched my arm, I closed my eyes and held my breath.

*Please don't go fishing. Please don't go fishing!*

"You can relax now," said the giant nurse. "We got it."

"Already?" The dark-red liquid pouring out of my arms and into the test tubes confirmed it. "Man! I didn't feel a thing!" A few minutes later, Giant Nurse came back into the room, holding a paper with the results.

"See you next week, Robert."

I didn't need Alicia to read the results. My mother a few years ago had hemoglobin of 6, and her organs started failing. I had to drive from Miami to Charleston, South Carolina, to take care of her. I spent a month in the hospital that year by her side.

"What's it say?" asked Mauricio on our way to the nutritionist.

"A 9."

"Okay...you're still alive, right?"

*That's right. Glory be to God...*

The nutritionist reviewed the diet plan. In her chipper voice, she was thrilled about the six pounds I gained. The scheduler put my next chemo for a week from now. If my hemoglobin was lower than 8, Kaywin would call for another blood transfusion.

After the hospital, we had lunch at Smoothie King, same thing: peanut butter, kale, weight gainer, and strawberries, added to their Hulk. Every day, since that first day, Mauricio and I would grab lunch there and go see the construction sites.

By the afternoon, driving back home, Mauricio finished his smoothie.

"I'll be out of town for a few days. I have to go see my mom in Jacksonville and check on her. It's been a while."

*C'mon, man! What the heck am I going to do without you here?*

"Okay. When will you be back?" I said, adjusting my seat. Pain was digging into my hip. I hated the idea of him leaving, not sure how I would go to hospital appointments and run the business without him driving me around. "You know I need you here."

He sighed. "I know. I already asked Alicia take over for a few days. I'm leaving tonight and will be back by midweek next week. She's done with her test already. So she has the time."

I remembered how it was dealing with two women who were exactly alike.

*Last man standing!*

"Well...hurry back!"

Alicia and Leila took me to the chemo appointment the next morning, after Mauricio had gone the night before. Like the two other chemos before it, I sat in the little chair at MCI, a nurse accessed my port, and when the medication arrived, a pump filled my port with the medicines. After three hours, we went home and I slept, waiting for the side effects.

By the second day, nausea and dry heaving were all I could focus on. I stuck to my recliner and dug my nails into the leather every time I felt a bout of nausea, trying to resist the urge to hobble to the toilet for nothing more than dry heaving.

Leila's skin was flushed and red; sweat was trickling down her neck and pooling at her collarbone, for a moment, dripping down her shirt. Her hands and face were still covered in dirt from gardening in the hot sun. That was our Saturday ritual; we both would do yard work and keep the front of the house looking pristine.

"Come out and get some sun with me, babe," she pleaded, serving herself a glass of ice tea and gulping it down in one go.

"It's okay," I said, shifting in my recliner. "You go. I'm not feeling so well today."

"Come on! The sun is shining, and there's not a cloud in the sky! Come help me do the weeds on the driveway." She held out her hand for me.

"I'll have Mauricio do them next week when he comes back, and the pool. It's bad enough he left."

"He has to see his mother too! He left his whole life up there to come down here!"

"Has Alicia gone to get my smoothie?" I asked, changing the subject.

"Yes, Robert." Leila sighed, giving up. "She'll be back soon, and you can spend the rest of your day sitting in that recliner."

The front door slammed on her way out. I curled up on the recliner and fell asleep. The TV had a Texas pastor preaching on God's restoration.

*Where is it?*

"Spapi...Spaaapi!" Alicia was shaking my shoulder. "Here's your smoothie." She handed me the oversize Styrofoam cup that took two hands to grab. I wasn't hungry, but I could feel the shaking in my organs getting more and more violent with each day.

*Hemoglobin must be going down.*

I took a sip of the banana, strawberry, and peanut butter cement. It would take me all day to sip this, thick as it was, but it was the only thing that kept my weight going up. Besides, I had nothing else to do.

Alicia sat on the step between the sunken living room and the dining room, a child-size smoothie on the floor next to her. "You know, Spapi, this is pretty good! I got the same one you did—without the weight gainer!"

"Yeah, it's pretty good. You heard from Mauricio yet? Did he make it up there okay?"

"Yeah, he's helping his mom put up a gate to the backyard so the dog doesn't run away."

"He-he-he! That kid's a mess, man!" I grabbed my stomach from laughing. "No permits? No inspections?"

"Just leave him alone!" she yelled, standing up. "He's doing the best he can! I'm sure it will turn out fine!"

"If you say so." I sipped my concrete, still chuckling, shaking my head.

"And by the way, you need to start walking!" She bent over me, arms on her hips. "Kaywin told you to start getting more active so new red blood cells can start forming. You haven't done it once since he told you. And you call *him* a mess?"

"Relax, Coos! It was a joke. I know you love to baby him."

"Baby him?" She started pacing around the living room, getting as red as her mother was from the sun. "He's with you every day he's here, taking you to the hospital, to your jobs, and even at home at night, when he has a quiet moment doing his thing in the boys' old room, you're calling him for no reason! And I baby him? I guess I have to, because he nonstop babies *you*!" she said, on the verge of tears. "And you won't even put any effort into what the doctor told you!"

Leila came in, hearing the shouting inside. Her arms crossed in the kitchen, not sure whether this situation would explode or settle down.

"Babe..." Leila stepped in. "All that Alicia is saying is that we both worry about you. The person in that recliner isn't you anymore. Don't you remember? How good it felt to be active and take care of our house together as a family?" She stepped forward next to Alicia, blocking the TV. "No one is asking you to mow the grass or clean the pool as you are, just to get out of that recliner and do something for yourself!"

*I need air!*

I grabbed my cane, hanging on the wall of the recliner. Slowly, with my legs shaking and my head throbbing, I walked past both of them, undoing the deadbolt to the back-yard, and stood there.

"Are you both finished?"

They nodded, following me.

"Ever since I was diagnosed, I've been afraid for my life. I've been afraid of the future where you won't have me around. I see myself in the mirror and I see a cadaver that moves and speaks and hobbles on a cane!" My throat hurt from speaking, but the rage and shaking in my body wouldn't stop. "You don't know what this is like. You have no idea! And while it's happening to our family, it's *my* body. I am constantly being eaten alive with pain! All the strength I had to lead men in construction is gone! I'm leaning on a cane and a young man to make me feel like there's at least another man in the house! I keep trusting in God's faithfulness and promise, and I don't feel it!"

Tears streamed down my face.

*They don't get it!*

"I have cancer!" I yelled at both of them, throwing my smoothie into the ground, splattering their feet, the walls, the cane, and the windows. "And no amount of sitting up straight or saying 'I feel good' will take that away!"

Everyone had tears on their faces now.

"Honey," said Leila, "I just don't see the future where we bury you!"

The rest of the weekend was black and miserable. Leila and Alicia barely spoke to me, except to bring me a smoothie at the recliner or give me a blood thinner shot in the belly. No one asked me to sit up straight anymore. For the next two days, I sat in my recliner during the day, and at night, Leila was already asleep by the time I went to bed.

It felt like something died out in the backyard. The mood was like at a funeral, everyone functioning, interacting, but without light in their eyes. Leila and Alicia spoke in low, hushed voices around the house, and barely at me. And when they did look at me, I saw it in their eyes.

*Hope had died.*

By Monday, Leila and Alicia ran errands. It was their way of getting out of the house and a break from me. I sat in my recliner, smoothie next to me, looking at the front door, wondering when they would be back. An hour passed. Then two. The blinds were closed, and even in the middle of the day, the den was dark. The battered emptiness inside me matched the den outside. Surrounded in that darkness, alone, I closed my eyes and talked to God.

"I know You told my wife I will not die of cancer. And I believe it. And I trust it. But, Lord, I sure don't feel like it! And I *sure* don't look like it!"

*You're not getting any better sitting in that chair.*

Every hair on my body stood on end. I heard a voice that sounded almost like my father's, or that of one of my brothers. It was a voice I knew my entire life, but I couldn't match it to a person. I looked around to see if anyone was there.

*Your wife's faith has carried you this far, but now it's up to you. You know the scriptures, "get up and walk!"*

I grabbed the cane on the wall again, shaking as bad as before, but I would not disobey this voice. One foot in front of the other, I walked from my recliner to the TV and back. Twenty paces total. I sat back down, breathless; pain jabbed into my lungs with every breath, but I was satisfied.

Keys jingled in the distance, the deadbolt clicked, and the front door showed Leila and Alicia carrying in groceries and our pressed dry-cleaning, wrapped in blue plastic sheets to protect from dirt.

"Leila?" I got up to meet them. Alicia kept walking to the kitchen to drop grocery bags on the counter. "Can we take a walk this evening?"

## First Prayer Night

The family hugged and kissed one another as they came in, gathering in the kitchen or in the living room in small pockets; some gathered around me in the recliner. Others were gathered on the couch or by the array of croquettes on the counter, talking about me.

"Oh my god! I had no idea he was so skinny!" I heard a cousin of Leila say, stealing glances in my direction. I smiled. I was used to it already.

"Yeah? It's been a tough five months." Smiled.

"I'm glad you called us, though! The whole family has been wanting to come see you guys and pray together."

"I know. He hasn't wanted anyone over until he got better."

"Is he?"

"We've been walking every evening. Maury or I join him for a walk along the street. Even getting to that was a battle. But whenever neighbors see us, they come to talk, and he always tells them, 'God has healed me.'" Leila took a sip of coffee. "So yeah, he's doing much better."

"How many chemos has he had?" asked Leila's niece, following the conversation.

"He's had five. One more to go and then they scan him and evaluate. That's happening in two days."

I cleared my throat. "Leila, are we ready?"

Leila gathered everyone into the den. Her parents sat next to me, Alicia next to them. Cousins took up the rest of the couch and the chairs that had been laid out for them.

"Guys, thank you for coming. It's been the fight of our lives these past few months." She paused, composing herself. "And I've gotten your calls and texts, even if I didn't reply to all of them. Thank you for praying for us. When Ana and Gisela came to see us last week, they came up with the idea to gather together and pray, believing in what the Bible says that 'when two or more are gathered, there He is.' And right now, we could use all the prayer we can get."

Leila, her cousin Rebecca, and her sister-in-law Cheryl took turns reading passages of Scripture. Between each speaker, Leila played worship songs. They reminded us that even in the middle of the storm, God did not let go of our hand. Alicia, and then Mauricio, read the final passages.

"Isaiah 53:4–5, 'Surely, he took up our pain and bore our suffering, yet we considered him punished by God, stricken by Him, and afflicted. But he was pierced for our transgressions, he was crushed for our iniquities, the punishment that brought us peace was on him, and by his wounds, we are healed.'"

Waves of goose bumps fell on me. My healing wasn't because of anything I did or could do; it was because of what He did. The price He paid to buy it. I wanted to weep, and hot tears ran down my cheeks.

"With that, let's hold hands and pray. Maury?" said Leila. Looking at Mauricio to start.

"Father, You know our hearts, and You have taught us that by including You in every situation, You only know how to turn it for good. What the devil meant for evil, You turn it for good. We thank You for Robert's life. We thank You for the price You paid for his healing through Jesus. We come together to thank You, asking as one that his healing be complete. That everyone who sees him sees You, and his life be a constant reminder of the work You've done in him."

I slapped the arms of the recliner. "Yes, Lord!"

When I opened my eyes, I saw the sticky note Leila put on the picture frame by the recliner. It came out of me, like a fire; either I screamed it or I would burst.

"I shall not die but live, and declare the works of the Lord!"

We all wept. Everyone came and prayed over me, some in groups of twos to threes, others by themselves. The most surprising one was my father-in-law. The man who, for years, had resentment toward anything from God walked over to me, bent over slowly, keeping his balance, and kissed me on the forehead.

"God bless you, chico. Be healed in the name of Jesus."
He sat by his wife again.

Leila closed the meeting with Carrie Underwood's rendition of "How Great Thou Art." It was the right song for a powerful night. But it meant more to her. She sat on the corner of the couch and bawled over, crying with everything she had inside of her. Her song came from a fully broken heart, one that had been stretched and mashed and beaten to a pulp, and still sang of God's greatness.

*Indeed, Father, how great Thou art...*

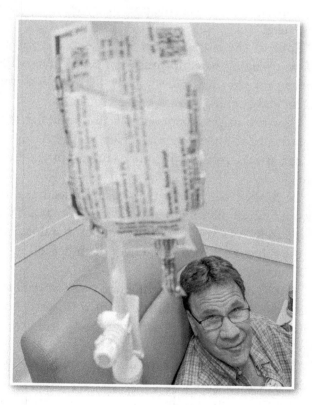

\*\*\*\*\*

By the time I walked into the infusion room, already three nurses and the receptionist greeted me by name. We had done all the necessary tests, and after another blood transfusion, Kaywin cleared me for the sixth chemo. Other nurses and techs that walked past my room stopped and said hello; they had been with me in one of the chemo sessions. Mauricio was on the chair next to me.

"Leila just texted," he said. "She wants you to text her at work when you're done."

"Barbara!" I waved to the tech coming my way, carrying heparin and saline to access the port in my leg. "God is good! I'm still here!"

"Robert!" she beamed. "Yes, He is! And yes, you are!"

I was playing worship music on my phone while the pharmacy got the medication ready. Barbara was putting gloves on and opening the syringe packages.

"I got my stripper pants on!" I said, undoing the buttons on the leg to show the port. "Hey, you guys don't mind the songs at this volume? I don't want to bother the other patients."

She flushed the port with saline, connecting the hose that would pump the chemo into my leg. "Not at all! We love jamming to it. And you're the only patient that does it. But I think the other patients like it. Gives them peace."

"Glory be to God!"

"Yeah! There's an older gentleman that comes here that's very depressed. I told him a little bit of your story, how you came in here with cancer all over your body, and how you're doing. It gave him hope."

"Tell everyone! They gave me six months to live, and look at me! God is good!"

I was quiet through the chemo, my eyes closed, praying and listening to the music blasting from my phone. I remembered my dad, who died of brain cancer when I was in my twenties. He was so light when I carried him from his bed to the car that last time. We drove to the hospital together. He never came home again.

"What's wrong?" asked Mauricio.

"My dad was my age when he died of cancer." The words of Kaywin rattled in my brain: *Let's hope you're still here by January.* It was October. Could I really beat the thing that took my dad from me?

"I shall not die but live, and declare the works of the Lord!" I shouted, startling Mauricio and the nurses at the station in front of my room. I didn't care; fear wouldn't eat me.

After the last bag of chemo finished, Barbara was flushing my port with heparin. "Okay, Robert, the next appointment is with Dr. Kaywin. The scheduler will make an appointment for a PET scan, and then he'll go over it with you!"

"How long will that be?"

"In about two weeks, give or take. I'm sure he wants to let this chemo do its job before sending for the scan."

That Sunday, our pastor gave a message on God's purpose in our lives. He brought the passage of Paul in Malta being shipwrecked and a poisonous snake biting his arm, and still he did not die. He just shook it off.

*Easy for Paul,* I thought. *He had an angel tell him he won't die until he speaks to Caesar. Where's my angel, Lord?*

The service ended with the announcement that Prophet Brian Carn would speak to the church the next Friday. That anyone with financial needs should come and hear him speak. Earlier that week, our insurance sent a statement of everything that had been paid for my treatment so far, well over two hundred thousand dollars! We were definitely going.

For the rest of the week, as we went to the jobs, or even to my walks with Leila, the nagging fear of not making it to

January clung to me, like that snake clung to Paul. "Shake it off!" I kept telling myself. It was easy to let my mind wander into the fear. The battle was in remembering God's promises. The peace in the bathroom, God's words to Leila, and then to Alicia, the family prayer night. I told this to Mauricio in the car on our way to a house we were remodeling.

"You have to remember, Rob, if He speaks to you, it's because He has a purpose in mind. It's normal to feel fear, especially with the sword dangling over your head. But it's in these moments, in spite of the fear, that you choose what to focus on. Do you focus on the fear? Or on what God told you? So when you feel this fear that you're going to die like your dad, what do you say?"

"Shake it off!"

"Shake it off!" he said.

Every day the battle continued. My jaw was itching like crazy, but I couldn't scratch it; the itch was under the skin, by the gums. My mouth felt differently every day, like every day was a new mouth that did not belong to me. There were moments where the pain eased, and I was able to sleep with Leila in the bed the whole night. Even our walks got longer. Last night we spent over half an hour walking the neighborhood. I was still out of breath, but nothing could keep me in that recliner anymore.

That Friday was a teacher workday. I had the final PET scan in the morning, and Leila went with me. It would determine if the chemo worked. Based on this information, Kaywin would decide if I needed to change medications or, in the worst case, go home and be comfortable.

"It'll be clear." I squeezed Leila's hand. She squeezed back. The machine roared, and even though the headphones and music dulled the noise outside, it was present. *It's still there,* came the thought.

*Shake it off!* I moved my lips, not making a sound. *This cancer is my serpent. I shake it off!*

\*\*\*\*\*

The church was filled with people coming to hear the prophet speak. Two thousand people, attentive, listening to this man give a message on supernatural provision. God, who provided all our needs according to His riches, would not forget us. Then he stopped.

Pacing the stage, over and over, he kept his head down, eyes closed. "The Holy Spirit stopped me," he said. "I don't know whom this is for, but God made you a promise. You will *not* die of cancer!"

*There's my angel!* I thought! Leila and I stood up and raised our hands in worship. "That's for me!" I shouted. "That's for me!"

Fear was there, but every step of the way, God showed me that He was there too. He showed me that He was worthy of my trust.

A few days later, I woke up with nausea and fatigue. They were familiar already; having gone through them so many times, I learned how to ignore the nausea. There was no ignoring the fatigue, not when you could feel your red blood cells die over and over. At five in the morning, Leila went to work and I went to nap in the recliner. I was dog-tired, but that just meant a longer walk this evening.

Around nine, the buzzing of my phone woke me up. It was the hospital. I turned the call off. Bad news could wait. It buzzed again. Off again. Mauricio hadn't woken up yet. I'd call the hospital when he woke up, and I didn't want to do it alone. My eyelids felt heavy, and I slept again. I heard the hum and trickle of running water first. He was finally up. I joined him in the kitchen and sat at the table. He took the seat across from me, still too sleepy to talk.

"Mornin'."

Before I could reply, my phone was buzzing again. It was Leila this time.

"Something must be wrong, man," I said, looking at the phone. "She never calls me while she's at work."

"Hello?"

"Hey, babe! Have you heard from Dr. Kaywin today?"

"No. I got a bunch of calls from the hospital, though."

"It's Dr. Kaywin. He's been trying to get ahold of you all morning! He couldn't wait to tell you, so he called me at work."

"Okay…"

"Your scans look great! Everything is gone. He said there are no new lesions, no new growths, and what was there got so small it's almost gone. You don't need any more chemo. He'll keep you on Keytruda for the time being, but this is it!"

"Babe?"

"Hello?"

"Are you there?"

# You Sit Here

*Maury*

He collapsed on the table. I could hear Leila's voice over the phone, trying to determine if he was still there. His back arched, and a deep, throaty moan emanated from within. Like a man on death row who expects an execution and, the day before it happens, is told he's going free instead. He wept for a while.

"Baby, are you there?" Leila said.

"I'm here! I'm here!" He gasped. "Oh my lord! Oh my god!" He wiped his eyes. "What else did he say?"

"That was it! He'll talk more at our next appointment and show us the scans!"

"Oh my god!" He cried.

"I can't believe it!"

"Me neither! Oh my god!"

"I love you so much. I gotta go! Stuart, I told you—"
She hung up.

"Thank You, Father! Thank You for my healing. Thank You for Your mercy and Your goodness. Thank You because You are a good, good God!"

He finally looked up at me, tears still streaming down his face. And smiled.

"Can you believe it? Glory be to God!" He pounded his fists on the dinner table.

"Tell Alicia we're going out to dinner tonight!" He walked to the middle of the living room and raised his hands to heaven. "Thank You, my Father! Oh, man, I have to call my mother!"

*****

We had been sitting at Kaywin's office for a few minutes now, waiting for him and his assistant to come in with the scans. Already we had done blood work and the usual measurements.

"You're doing great, babe. You're at 172, and you hemoglobin is at 10!"

"Bimyow!" yelled Robert, picking a booger off his nose on the exam table.

"Don't stick it on the table!" yelled Leila.

"They throw away the paper after every patient, anyways!"

Before they could continue fighting about proper booger placement, the door swung open. Kaywin and his assistant, Shannon, came in holding scans.

"Look at this guy!" said Kaywin, pulling out his stethoscope. "It's amazing! You guys must be thrilled." Shannon took notes on the computer while Kaywin listened to Robert's lungs.

"Oh my goodness!" said Leila, "I wish I could hear it again! You caught me by surprise at school." She laughed.

Kaywin took a chair next to Robert. "So these are the reports of the scan. There's what's called mixed response. Every target node, hip, brain, spine, jaw, and lung has either been completely removed or is significantly smaller. The only spot that we have to keep a watch on that doesn't fit with everything else is the adrenal gland."

Robert took a sip from his water bottle, following along as best as he could.

"They call it mixed response if the right adrenal is proved to be metastatic. We don't know for sure. It could just be inflammation. So like I said, some of these areas haven't gone away completely, but we're keeping an eye on them to determine if they're inflammation. You haven't had any fevers lately, have you?"

"No," said Robert and Leila at the same time.

"Good. Every place is showing improvement by decreasing in size or heat signature coming from the masses. It's not a complete response. It's not like everything is back to normal. But I wasn't expecting that either. But compared to where you are from where you were, the difference is extraordinary."

"So when can we get rid of it?"

"Well, we're working on that!"

"We're gonna get rid of it!"

Leila laughed.

"As far as your jawbone," continued Kaywin, "the scans showed the bone is healing nicely, so I wouldn't recommend radiating that spot right now."

"Is Keytruda working on that?"

"Yes. You tested high for Keytruda responsiveness, and that means it's working well throughout your body, so we're going to keep you on it. We're going to make another appointment for an MRI for November, and your next Keytruda is on the ninth."

*Sounds good!* Robert said, "Leila? What chu doin', honey?" Hearing the rapid-fire clicking of a phone keyboard.

"Texting my family! We're having another prayer night, this time to thank God."

## Second Prayer Night

Croquettes and mini ham sandwiches were disappearing from the trays and into the grabby hands of hungry family members. I saw Alicia buried in aunts as she tried to get to the kitchen for water; at one point only her hands and her head were above the crowd.

"Oh my gosh, Robert! Look at you!" shouted Roxana with glee. "You look so good!"

"Glory be to God!" He kissed her cheek, on his left side. His right had returned to normal, except for a fold of skin that looked like an unfortunate scar from a bad bar fight.

I liked the scar; it added character to his face.

Noticing her eyes glance over his chin, he smiled. "It's my Jacob scar," he joked. "Jacob fought with the angel and limped for the rest of his life. I fought too. And we both got our blessing."

If nothing else, every time he looked in the mirror, he would remember what God did for him.

"Okay, guys, let's sit! We can eat the rest later!" yelled Leila, in her teacher voice, trying to make herself heard over the hum of the crowd in her kitchen. It worked. Before long, everyone was seated on the couch, on folding chairs laid out for the occasion.

"Some of you were here a few weeks ago, when we didn't know if we would ever get to this point. All we knew was that my husband was going to die." Her voice started shaking. "We had no other choice than to turn it all to God. There was no plan B." Tears started to well in her eyes. She smiled. "I'm sorry!" She laughed. "God has been good to us. My husband right here is living proof that He heard our prayers."

The broken-vacuum-cleaner noise coming from the recliner told everyone that Robert shared his wife's feelings. He slapped his knee. "God is so good!"

Leila continued, "We learned quickly through this process that it's consuming. All-consuming. It takes over the body, but also over your life. The cancer now dictates your reality. It paralyzes you with fear that you'll lose your husband, robs us of our future, and drains everything—energy, finances...joy. It's a mess!"

"Yes, it is!" shouted Robert. Everyone else nodded in agreement.

"Then God shows up! In the middle of that hot mess, we learned that He doesn't spare you the pain but will walk it with you. One of the things He told us was to trust Him. Fully trust Him. And it's hard to imagine a happy ending when we see one problem after another. It's hard not to be angry when time goes by, and we lose ground instead of gaining it. Even then, He kept saying it: 'Trust in Me.'"

Her hands trembled, holding the paper. Alicia squeezed my hand tight. Like her mom, she knew the gravity of those words. And how hard it was to do.

"It took a while, but we saw God's hand in the storm. Even now, between us four, we look at one another and go, 'How did we get through this?'"

"It had to be God!" said Alicia.

"So now, we want to tell Him, 'Thank You!' You guys saw us at our lowest point, and now we get to share the good stuff together."

We worshipped that night. His presence moved in the house, filling the walls with peace. Since the first night, when Alicia told me about his diagnosis, He had shown me that He never let go of us.

## Thanksgiving

Thanksgiving was the first holiday we celebrated together. The smell of roast turkey and thyme filled Cheryl's house when we walked in. Rey carved the wild-caught turkey, placing slices of light and glistening dark meat on a platter for the buffet table. The turkey was surrounded by cranberry salad, roast brussels sprouts, and sweet potato casserole—marshmallows and all.

"Oh, man! Sweet-tater casserole!" yelled Robert, eyeing the orange marshmallow dish greedily. Coming up behind me and throwing an arm around my shoulder.

"Dude! Could you be more of a redneck?" I said, wrapping an arm around his back, tightening into an awkward half-hug.

"I reckon! Ya dang foreigner!"

We both laughed.

*Yes. Yes, he could.*

There wasn't enough space in the house to accommodate the fifty people present. Tables and chairs were set on the grass. Bistro lights, big as Christmas ornaments, were strewn between the branches in the backyard, bathing the tables in a warm glow. Alicia and I sat with cousins around our own age group. Behind us was another table, where Robert, Leila, her parents, and her aunts were seated.

"This is delicious!" I could hear Robert say. "I haven't had an appetite since April!"

"What did you eat all those time?" asked Mercy, Leila's aunt, sipping a glass of Merlot.

"Nothing," said Leila, giving her husband a chance to chew between questions.

"Because of the cancer in my jaw, I couldn't eat anything. I couldn't chew!"

"What did you do?"

"Smoothie King was a lifesaver! Mauricio and I would go every day there for lunch. I had them make me a smoothie with enough calories to keep my weight. I needed 3,500 calories a day, just to not lose weight!"

"He bothered the poor cashier so much that they named the smoothie after him," I interrupted.

"You're kidding!" said Mercy. "How much do you weigh now?"

"It was easier than saying every ingredient in the thing, anyways. About 175. I was in the 140s."

"Amazing! What's it called?"

"The Robert!" He laughed. "If you go to the Smoothie King on Bird and Eighty-Seventh and ask for a Robert, you'll get a bucket-size smoothie, thick as concrete, that weighs about three pounds!"

"No, thank you!" said Mercy, taking another sip of wine. "And are you completely off treatments?"

"I still have Keytruda. My oncologist, Dr. Kaywin, doesn't want to take me off it for now. But I'm off chemo." Taking another bite of turkey with sweet potatoes.

## Oral Surgeon

During the last checkup, at the end of November, Kaywin recommended an appointment with the oral surgeon on his team, to see if Robert could get his three teeth back. Alicia was working, so I joined Robert and Leila in their appointment.

"I want to start with a biopsy to make sure there's no cancer in the bone," said the doctor, not looking up from his chart. "Then we can cut out the cancerous jaw and take a piece of your femur, or your rib, and make another jaw from there. Once it gets into the bone, it never leaves."

"Is all that really necessary? Dr. Kaywin said the jaw is healing okay," said Leila, crossing her arms. "Besides, it's been our experience that with God, anything is possible."

"Mrs. Germroth, once cancer gets in the jaw, he's a goner in four months. Tops." The oral surgeon stood up and examined Robert's mouth. "Say 'Aaaaaah."

*Oh no, he did* not *just say that!*

"He's right in front of you!" said Leila, fuming.

"Ma'am," said the doctor, holding up his gloved hand, "I'm trying to do what's best for your husband. It's not like I need the money from the operation. I'll set an appointment for the biopsy."

"That's nice," said Robert, getting up from the exam table. "You go ahead and do that. But nobody is cutting into me until I speak to Dr. Kaywin." Robert opened the door and left.

I held the door open for Leila, who grabbed her purse, turned to leave, and suddenly stopped.

"And by the way, Doctor," she said, smiling, "it's November. He was diagnosed in April. Do the math. He's still here. Next time, try a little sensitivity."

As we drove home, Robert had Kaywin on speaker.

"No, no! I don't feel comfortable with him!"

"I agree. Don't do anything with this guy anymore. Your jaw looks good, and keep in mind, your jaw healed around the implants that were installed. Cutting that open and messing with it is more trouble than it's worth."

"Okay. So no biopsy, then?"

"No. Robert, Leila, don't worry. I'll take care of it. You won't hear from this guy again."

He hung up with Kaywin, adjusted his glasses, and smiled.

"Okay, Leila, go!" Seeing his wife about to burst.

"Can you believe this guy?" she screamed. "I mean, of all the things a doctor could say to a patient inches from him. Inches!" The leather steering wheel cracked under her hands.

Robert laughed, caressing her thigh.

"Honey, you tore into that guy!"

"And who mentioned money? Did you catch that?"

"No idea. But you were fierce!"

She laughed, grabbing his hand. "Yeah. I don't know where that came from!"

"That was kinda sexy."

"Really?" She was not amused.

"Really?" I yelled from the back seat. "I'm right *here*!" Laughing. Robert slapped his hand on his thighs. Leila laughed so hard she snorted.

By mid-December, the house had been overtaken by Christmas decorations. The neatly manicured lawn, with sensible palm trees and crushed limestone, sported light-up reindeer, candy cane spikes, and a trail of crimson bows leading to the front door. Fading pine needles still dotted the walkway, belonging to the tree Robert and I lugged into the house. The tree stood on one corner of the sunken living room, and sprouting from it, boxes and boxes, of all shapes and size, filled the living room. I had never seen so many presents in a single room before that were not mall decorations. Leila had gone nuts.

The jobs had finished for the year, and the only thing left was a final blood work appointment with Shannon, Kaywin's assistant, and Keytruda, before Robert and Leila traveled to South Carolina. Walking into the exam room, Robert was unusually quiet.

"You nervous about this meeting?" I asked, opening the door to the exam room so we could walk in. "You know you don't have to be. Look how far you've come!"

"Huh?" His eyes glazed.

"Never mind."

"No, I'm not nervous about this. I was thinking about my mother. It's the first time I'll see her since I was diagnosed."

"Ah, right. I forgot about that."

"With so much that's happened, I didn't think I would get to see her."

Shannon walked in. "Hey, Robert! Happy holidays! Dr. Kaywin is already traveling with his family, so I'll be taking a look at you."

Shannon listened to his lungs, felt his throat for lumps, and pulled up the latest scans on the computer. He flipped the screen, showing black-and-white outlines of his head, and another MRI image of his torso.

"Well, you look great! Everything we've been keeping an eye on is decreasing or gone. I think the only thing that we're iffy about is the spot on the adrenal gland. Has Dr. Kaywin said anything about that?"

"He said he wasn't terribly worried, inflammation maybe. If it's not inflammation, he says they could zap it with radiation."

"That's right. Okay, well, again, you look great. Have a happy holidays and be safe if you're traveling."

As he was about to turn off the computer, I stopped him.

"Wait! Go back to the scan of his head for a second!" I took out my phone and took a picture.

"What's up?" Robert asked. "What did you see?"

"Oh, nothing. Just getting proof you have a brain!"

Shannon and Robert laughed. Before Shannon left, Robert asked him, "Hey, Shannon, did you think I'd make it this far?"

He stopped for a second, pursing his lips. Unsure of how to proceed.

"Honestly? No. I was very surprised at how well you've responded to the medicine."

Robert laughed and pointed a finger to the ceiling. "Glory be to God."

"Glory be to God," he said, imitating Robert. He quickly said his goodbyes and left; I'm sure that was not a conversation he was keen on continuing.

I threw an arm around Robert as we crossed the hall to the exit.

"Now you can go see your mom!"

## Christmas Eve

Christmas Eve, we spent it with Doris, at Leila's mom's side of the family.

"We're late!" yelled Alicia, squeezing next to me in the half-bath to apply eye shadow in the mirror above the sink.

"I'm shaving!"

"I need the mirror!"

Decades ago, to make the minuscule bathroom look bigger, her parents covered two of the four walls in floor-to-ceiling mirrors.

"Pick a wall!" I yelled. "I need the sink!"

"Babe! Hair is falling everywhere! Move!"

"I'm shaving!" I said defensively. "Fine! We'll clean up the hair on the floor later!" I conceded to shave in front of the mirror wall until she finished. Robert's reflection appeared in the mirror behind me.

"Mauricio..." He looked serious.

*Oh god.*

"Dude, don't you think it's a little weird for two grown men to talk in a tiny bathroom without shirts on?"

He smiled.

"Well, it's about to get weirder. I need you to shave my neck with that thing you're holding there." He pointed to the electric razor.

I looked around the hall to make sure Alicia was nowhere in sight; she wouldn't let me live this down.

"Get in!"

And there I was, behind my girlfriend's dad, both of us topless, in a minuscule bathroom, shaving the curly hairs on his neck. It would have been bad enough that the mirror above the sink showed his face, so even with me behind him, we still made eye contact. But it was so much worse! The floor-to-ceiling mirrors next to us and behind me gave us every painful awkward angle of the exchange.

It couldn't get any worse.

From her room, I heard the cackle of my girlfriend losing it. She came out, in her green Christmas blouse and jeans, laughing so hard her face was turning red.

I was wrong.

"Don't move! Don't move! I have to take a picture of this!"

"No! No, no, no! No, you don't!"

Robert started laughing at this too. Shaking his neck in the process.

"C'mon, man! I'm almost done!" I said, holding his shoulders so he wouldn't move. "NO! DON'T YOU TAKE THAT PICTURE!"

"Too late! This is gold. I got to show Mami!" She ran off to her mother's bathroom.

"I hate you," I said under my breath.

"Me or her?"

I paused for a second. Wiping the loose hair from his neck with a towel.

"Yes."

Doris's relatives loved to celebrate. If there was an opportunity to get together, eat, drink, and dance, they were on it. They reminded me of my own family, sharing the "Life is short, eat the croqueta" philosophy. At their house, several tables were lined together in the backyard, and two inside to accommodate all the guests. No one knew how many people were there. Cuban parties had that quality. When asked the question, "How much food or drink should we have?" the answer was always the same: "Enough."

In the corner of the yard, two guys dug a pit and were roasting a whole hog with banana leaves. Embers sizzled as droplets of fat melted and dripped on them, sending sparks. They had been there since morning, taking turns.

"Oh my goodness! This is delicious, man!" said Robert, grabbing another bite of rice and black beans.

"Yeah. Ever since the cancer, he's been eating everything in sight," said Leila to her cousins. "Now we have to go out to dinner every night! And that's great. He's gaining weight but making the rest of us fat in the process."

Robert was done with his plate and was nibbling bites of Leila's leftover pork while she told relatives the story of his recovery.

"And he's cancer-free?"

"Yes!" he said with a mouthful of pork before Leila could answer. "In the name of Jesus, I am healed!"

Leila nodded.

After dinner, I sat in the backyard under the lights, nuzzling bourbon and listening to Alicia's grandfather tell stories of Cuba in Spanish. Robert sat next to me.

"You okay?" he asked. "This old man bothering you?"

"Nah. I like the stories. They remind me of my childhood."

"Can you believe it, Mauricio?" he asked, expecting me to read his mind.

"Yeeees?"

He smiled. "Can you believe how far God has brought us four? He took me from a cigarette-smoking, pot-smoking workaholic that was about to die from cancer all over his body. He healed me, brought my wife, my daughter, and me closer to Him. I wasn't walking with Him before, but now our family is seeing what God did in me, and we're able to talk to them about God."

I smiled, sipping more bourbon.

"It's amazing, man," he continued. "I was going to die. He gave me my life back."

"No, He didn't," I said. "He didn't heal you for you to be the same person. You would have never survived. You're not the same guy I met when we talked in the backyard of your house by the pool."

"You're right. He's been so good and so merciful. There are no words."

I sipped the last of the bourbon.

*You really are, Lord.*

## Christmas Day

The smell of pancakes wafting in below the door of Alicia's room got us out of bed. Before I could finish stifling a yawn, Alicia had already raced past the boxes of presents in the living room and to the kitchen, where Robert cooked breakfast.

"They better be on the couch!" I heard Alicia tell her mom. "You've been doing that since I was two!"

"I had to do that so they could be at eye level. You're a grown woman now."

"Doesn't matter! It's tradition!"

I walked into the den to find Alicia hopping on the couch, a stack of presents next to her.

"Come on, babe!" She held out her hands. "Let's open presents!"

"Well, merry Christmas to the rest of us too!" I said, ignoring her, joining Robert in the kitchen instead. "Need help?"

"Git away!" he said, swatting me with a greasy spatula from the sausages he was burning in the pan. "It's my day! One day a year, on Christmas, I cook breakfast! Not you, not Leila, and certainly not Alicia—me! And with the year like I had, nobody is taking it away from me!" He pointed to a paper plate on the counter. "Biscuit?"

Tearing off bits of the biscuit, I sat on the floor by Alicia, trying to peek into her presents.

"Look, babe! You got presents!" She pointed to a pile next to hers, equally large. "Can we open them already?" she begged her mom, who had just set a gallon of Aunt Jemima on the table.

"Babo and Baba are coming any minute. We'll wait for them!"

"You guys have everything ready for South Carolina?" I asked.

"Yep!" said Robert, pouring the blackened sausages on a paper plate. "We're hittin' the road as soon as we're done wrapping presents today." He turned his hips back and forth into a weird dance, singing, "I'm gonna see my mother, I'm gonna see my motheeer, na na na ni boo boo!"

Alicia didn't have to wait long; Babo and Baba were walking into the house fast enough to catch the end of Robert's shimmy.

"No one should see that, *mijo*," she told him, giving him a peck on the cheek. Before Babo had said his hellos, she was already seated at the table, with a piece of pancake in her mouth.

"Okay, Alicia, *go!*" said Leila.

"YAAASSS!"

Flurries of wrapping paper flew across the den, bouncing off the footrest and barely missing the lamp.

"Omigod, babe, oh mah god!" Her feet were stomping as she held blue pajamas with dachshunds printed on them. "Yaaaaas!"

"Open this one next!" said Leila, handing her a rectangular box.

More wrapping paper flew everywhere. This time hitting Baba on the shoulder as she sat in the recliner, ready to open her own presents.

"Weiner slippers! Mami, where did you find these?"

"Amazon." Leila smiled. "I found them when I was searching for Maury's gifts, and I just had to get them for you."

"I love them! Look, babe!" She held out her feet inches from my face. "When you put the feet together, they make a wiener doggie!"

It was easy to forget she held people's lives in her hands at work every day.

After all the gifts were opened, Robert looked at Leila, who was clipping a new Pandora charm to her bracelet.

"Did you like your presents, babe?"

"Come with me." She grabbed his hand and led him to the living room, which was still full of presents for friends. "Maury, you come too! Bring your phone!"

190

She grabbed a green bow from one of the gift boxes and stuck it on his chest. An elf hat from the collection on the couch, and he stuck it on his head. "You sit here!" She pointed to a clear spot between the presents beneath the tree.

"Maury, take a picture of the only gift I want this Christmas."

"Speaking of pictures, I haven't given you guys my present!" Alicia brought out a thin square box from beneath the tree.

"I didn't know what to get you guys that you don't already have. But I hope this makes up for it."

Robert tore the wrapper and pulled out a thin book with a picture of them on the cover, reading a newspaper and a book.

"A Healing in Progress? What is it?"

"Just look at it."

We were all sitting on the floor among the presents. Robert and Leila sat cross-legged, eyeing every photo in the book.

"So that's why you were always on your phone!" said Leila, welling up.

"Look at this, babe! He took pictures of me sleeping!"

"It's more than that. I wanted you to remember what God rescued you from. It's my way of documenting the work He's done in your lives."

Robert stood up, and Leila followed. He wrapped his arms around me tight and cried, which made my eyes sting. "You're my son!" he said, holding on tighter. "God brought you into our lives for a purpose, at just the right time. You're my son!"

Leila and Alicia wrapped their arms around us too. We stayed there for a long time, buried in the embrace.

"Oh, I can't wait to show this to my mother!" he said, wiping his eyes.

"Dad, Mom, come see this!" Leila called to Babo and Baba.

## Sunday at Church in January

Word got around church that the old man with a cane wasn't wearing a cane anymore. A very tall woman approached

Robert before service, tapping him on the shoulder and stopping us in the middle of the lobby.

"Excuse me. You used to have a cane, right?"

"Oh yeah!" He smiled. "Until my wife made it disappear while I was on the toilet."

"You didn't need it!" said Leila. "You just needed help realizing that. I just nudged. Gently."

"I don't know if you remember," said the tall woman. "Pastor Mariam had me pray over you once, when she made an altar call and you walked up." She smiled. "Your face was swollen, and you were afraid for me to touch your jaw."

"I remember. My doctor said that the bone was so fragile it could break at any second."

"You were so skinny!" she beamed. "But now you look so good! I'm Martha!" she said, shaking hands with both of them. "My husband, Robert, and I run the intercessory prayer group before service. We were praying for you."

"Oh my goodness! Martha, thank you both so much! Glory be to God! You have no idea what that means." He pulled out his phone. "Over Christmas, my daughter's boyfriend made us a book of pictures of my recovery. I had him put them on my phone to show people!"

"Oh, wow! People need to see this! What a testimony!" she said.

I pulled Alicia aside. "Let's save them seats. It looks like they'll be here a while." There were many more people than usual in the lobby. "Do you know what's going on?"

"I think the new pastor is starting today."

"What's his name?"

A few days later, we were back at the hospital for a dentist's appointment. The blond dentist examined his implants, writing notes in her chart. Robert gargled and spit on the silver drain by his head after every test she conducted.

"And you're aware of the situation with my jaw?" he asked her, sitting up after she had finished.

"Absolutely. Dr. Kaywin was very thorough when he called. We took a look at the latest scans. There is no cancer in your jaw, and the bacterial environment in your gums looks good."

"Kaywin said not to mess with the implants since the bone and gums healed around them even though they are crooked."

"Right, they moved as your mouth healed. One of them is completely fallen over. We can put a bridge, with the missing teeth, to fill the gap."

"So I'm okay?" he asked, falling back into the exam chair.

"You're okay!" She smiled.

"He's taking care of everything. Every little thing, He's taken care of."

"Who?"

"God. Last April, doctors told me they had no cure, that I might not be here in January. Crazy!"

Dinner that evening was just the three of us. Alicia was working nights, so she mostly slept during the day and left for work by 5:00 p.m. Robert spooned more garbanzo beans onto his plate, mixing it evenly with the rice. Leila sipped ice tea and said nothing. The repetitive click of metal on porcelain, devoid of conversation to mask it, echoed throughout the house.

"I was gone for a few hours. What did I miss?"

"Nothin'," said Robert, sipping ice tea.

"Can I tell him?"

"Is it cancer? Is it back?"

They both looked taken aback. Leila smiled.

"No. Things are great, thank God! Leila's just being airheaded."

"Oh, this is silly, Robert!" she said, slamming her glass on the table. Before he could interrupt, she held a hand to his face. "I've been keeping for Alicia a wedding ring that belonged to her great-grandmother. No pressure at all. I know you and Robert have to talk. But if you want to use it, we want you to have it."

"Not we!"

"Okay!" Leila conceded. "I…I want you to have it! If you want it! Don't answer now, just think about it."

Since we started dating, I measured Alicia's relationship against every other relationship I had ever had. Every past relationship, in their own way, taught me what to look for. Each terminated romance was a signpost bringing me closer to the one I needed to be with. The heartbreak of my parents' divorce, my earliest lesson, taught me the importance of picking the right person. One wrong decision could devastate multiple lives for years, but the opposite is also true: the right decision restores and builds for generations to come. Alicia was my right decision.

"Can I talk now?" asked Robert, pushing his empty plate away.

"Go ahead."

"What he doesn't know is that the ring also belonged to you in your first marriage."

"So? It's a beautiful ring, and Alicia would have loved her great-grandmother! She was named after her."

"It's the ring of a failed marriage! It's tainted!"

"It wasn't the ring's fault he cheated!"

"All I'm saying is, he should know all the facts!"

He threw his arms in the air. "Like Leila said, don't answer now."

Out the window, the sky was purple, and orange clouds streaked through it, reflecting the last rays of the sun.

"Come on, Leila, we're late for our walk. I may need you to translate to the neighbor next door. He doesn't speak English but points to the sky every time he sees me."

January 11, we were back at MCI for Keytruda. Every three weeks, like clockwork, Robert and I would spend most of the morning there. We knew the drill by now, blood work (fine), weight (181.2), and a forty-five-minute infusion through the port in his leg.

Taking the chair next to him, I checked paperwork for a new job building a massive covered terrace for a new client.

"This thing is going to be tricky. There isn't enough space to get a crane in the yard, so we're going to have to fly those trusses by hand when we're building the roof," he said.

Spending enough time running errands for him between jobs, I learned that trusses were like the skeleton system of the roof. Normally, a single truck carried the entire system and dropped the colossal wooden triangles, wide as a house, for a crane to lift them into position.

"So you're telling me that you want me and three guys in their fifties to lift trusses fourteen feet in the air by hand?"

"Yes. Don't forget, they weigh between six and eight hundred pounds each."

*Wonderful!*

"And how do you expect us to do this?"

He laughed. "Philippians 4:13, buddy."

I opened my laptop again, checking e-mail. "By the way, did Leila tell you?" I asked him.

"Tell me what?"

"Alicia wants to move out."

## Not Living in Sin

A few days ago, after her parents were asleep, she came into my room. We both squeezed onto the trundle bed she used as a child, her wet hair soaking into my Power Rangers pillow.

"We're not happy here, babe."

"We're not? Really?"

"Look at my dad—he's okay! We should be able to start our lives!"

"You mean they haven't?"

She smacked my shoulder.

"You know what I mean! I grew up hearing, 'Once you get your license and you get your job, you can have your own place.' Well, I did that! Now we should have our own place!"

The Keytruda pump started beeping as I finished telling Robert the story. He started laughing.

"Tag. You're it! That's my daughter, Mauricio. She's always been impatient. Nothing ever came quick enough for her. In her fifth birthday party, she was angry she wasn't six already."

"You're not helping, old man!"

"She and Leila have been butting heads lately. Don't ask me about what, and don't you get involved! Or you're the bad guy."

The nurse came in and flushed his port. I left the room and drew the curtain so he could change from stripper pants to jeans.

"Maybe she's right." He cleared his throat. "Maybe y'all do need your own place already. She did do everything we asked, the only kid that actually did."

He drew back the curtain.

"But I'll tell you, I don't like the idea of you two living together without being married. That's living in sin."

We drove to Smoothie King, making the line without looking at the menu board. The same cashier that took our order when we first pulled in was there, yelling orders to the guys behind him over the roar of commercial blenders. Seeing us, he yelled.

"Strawberry protein and a Robert!"

"Heard!" came the reply.

"Dude, you look so good!" yelled the cashier.

"Dude, I had cancer all over my body! God healed me."

"Dude!" The cashier threw his arms in the air.

"I'll tell you, though," said Robert, grabbing the smoothies, "these have been a lifesaver for me!"

"Well, thank God, dude!"

"Glory be to God!"

He yelled that so often, in church, in the shower, in Chuck Wagon at breakfast, in the office to his computer, that you learned to live with it. There was no quiet room safe from Robert—he would fill the space yelling his praises.

"Let's go," I said, grabbing him by the elbow, "before they make that a drink too."

"Dude!" they both yelled.

Over the next week, Leila started bringing boxes from work, and Alicia would fill them. Every time we came home from the job, there would be more and more boxes filling up the sunken living room.

"This is driving Leila nuts," whispered Robert in my ear, unsure of who was home.

"She doesn't want us to go?"

"No, she hates the mess in her living room!"

No one was home yet. We sat at his desk in the office, where he first showed me the business, thinking he would die from peeing blood.

"Rob?"

"Hmm?" He was deleting spam e-mails, one by one.

"I know we haven't talked about this, but it's important to me. You're the man in her life, and it won't happen without your blessing." I gulped. "Can I marry your daughter?"

*Click. Click. Delete.*

"Hello?"

"Acknowledge."

He swiveled in his office chair. "Mauricio, there's no doubt in my mind you're going to marry my daughter." He put a hand on my shoulder. "My only question is, you sure?"

I nodded. "Yes, sir."

He giggled, a gleeful, creepy giggle. Swiveling back to the computer. "I can't wait to tell Leila! We found the fool!"

"Come again?" I made him face me again.

"Leila and I always told Alicia when she was being a pain, 'I pity the fool that marries you.' Now we found the fool!"

I cooked dinner that evening. Alicia had to work, so it was just the three of us. The smell of coconut rice filled the kitchen as Leila set the table. By the time I set the shrimp, braised cabbage, and pot of sticky coconut rice on the table, she had already nudged Robert to sit and was the first to spoon a heaping clump of rice on her plate.

"Okay, Leila," Robert said, bracing himself for a fight. "Let's talk about the ring you have for Alicia."

"We found the foo?" she asked, excitedly.

"Sure did!"

"Yay!" She threw her arms around my neck and squeezed.

"Focus, woman!"

She turned to Robert. "It has a lot of sentimental value. I know it would mean a lot to Alicia to get it."

"Still think it's cursed."

"Hold on, Rob," I interrupted. "You just got through cancer, you saw God's hand on your life, and you think a piece of rock has the power to destroy a marriage?"

"Exactly!" said Leila with a mouthful of rice. "And if there's something wrong with the ring, we pray and believe that God is stronger than curses or bad juju or whatever!"

"We'll need to get a new setting," said Robert finally.

"Oh yeah! That one is from the eighties! The setting is hideous!"

*****

The weight of the truss dug into my shoulder, rubbing it raw. Being careful not to slip on mounds of dirt or fall into the pool, Eddie, Tino, and Alfredo walked the massive wooden triangles to the back of the house. Once there, Tino and Alfredo would climb up on the roof and wait for Eddie and me, one on each end, to hoist the wooden framework up.

"Good!" yelled Robert from the roof. "Just seven more to go! This was the hard one. Let's go!"

After Tino and Alfredo secured the truss, they would go down and we would all walk the next one. And the next. And the one after that.

"Tino, don't you let it fall! You'll kill somebody!" barked Robert. Tino nailed boards between the trusses to hold one another.

We were exhausted at the final truss. Sweat dripped down to our ankles, and despite the gloves, my hands were covered in blisters.

"Watch out with this one!" Robert yelled. "This is the heavy one!"

"What the heck were the other ones, then?" I yelled. "You said it would get easier!"

"I lied! Watch that window, Alfredo!"

Once the last truss was up, Robert was on the ground, making sure the peaks in the trusses lined up. There was no room for error; if they didn't align, the roof would leak later.

"Eddie, a little to the left! NO, my left!" he said.

"Mauricio! Bring your end a little closer to the edge. We can't have a gap!"

I lifted my corner on my shoulder, my spine compressed from the weight, and splinters tore into my shoulder, inching the forty-foot reinforced triangle closer to the edge of the concrete beam it was sitting on.

"Closer!"

"A little more! Come on, man! When I was your age, I could do this with one hand!"

*Lord, either You take him or I send him...*

"That's it! Bimyow!"

We leaned against the wall of the house, trying to catch our breath, furiously gulping water.

"Come on, wannabe! We're done for today. Let's beat the traffic."

"Wannabe?" asked Eddie.

"He's my wannabe son-in-law!"

Driving home, Robert handed me a water bottle. My shirt was sticking to me with sweat.

"You nervous?"

"Not till you asked me."

He laughed.

"You don't have to be."

"Were you?"

"I planned a picnic for us. I was going to take her to the park, and she would find the ring in a little apple-shaped ring box, since she's a teacher. She found it in the drawer before we left. My heart was in my throat the whole time. I couldn't say the words. She just said yes and kissed me."

We took the ring to the jeweler the next day. They removed the diamond from Leila's old engagement ring, polished it, and in a ring of white gold with a four-pronged setting, turned it into Alicia's ring. Robert and I held it in our hands. He smiled.

"I always told Alicia when she was growing up, 'If any boy asks me to marry you, the first thing I'll say is, "Show me the ring,' and if it's a cheap, gumball-machine ring, I'd tell him to turn around and try again.'"

"Wow."

"You dog! You got me to go with you and pick it out."

"Can't mess up that way." I smiled. "By the way, how did you know Alicia's ring size?"

"The tip of my pinkie!" He laughed. Putting on the ring. "Leila borrowed a ring from her, and I tried it on to get the size. How did you find out?"

"She mentioned it once last, and I wrote it down."

"That's not creepy at all."

"Says the ring stealer."

He laughed, slamming his hand on the glass counter-top, shaking the rings below.

"How are you going to do it? Just you and her?"

"We've had a very hard year, Rob. We shared some really difficult times together. I think we should share something good also, no?"

He smacked me on the bruised shoulder a few times, sending shocks of pain to my feet.

"You're a good kid, Mauricio."

## Look Down

The restaurant buzzed, waiters carrying bottles and glasses of champagne whizzed past families engrossed in conversation. The whole place carried a low hum dotted with faint pops of a champagne bottle being opened.

"Happy birthday, sweetie," said Baba, handing Alicia a small square gift bag and a kiss.

"I love this perfume!" she said, sniffing the neck of the bottle. "Look, Mami!"

Sitting across from each other, Leila and my mom both smelled the perfume.

"This is a really nice place!" said Alicia, looking around at the ornate abstract sculptures separating the tables.

"Ye-yeah!" I smiled.

"What are you guys having?"

"We're waiting for Robbie, Nicole," said Leila. "They were in town and wanted to share your birthday."

"Well, finally, I get to share a birthday with my brother!"

"Carlos too."

"He's coming?"

"Yeah. He wouldn't miss your birthday for the world."

"Where are they?" asked Robert, looking at the entrance.

"Any minute now," I said, looking at my watch. "Any minute now."

Our waiter passed by, bringing an old-fashioned and setting it by my hand. Before anyone else said anything, he was gone already. After a few minutes, the rest of the party showed up.

"By the way, babe, why were you asking me about rings earlier?"

"I forgot what style ring you like. When I propose, I want to make sure I have the right one."

"Can we order? I'm starving!" said Alicia, eyeing the menu. "Oooh, lamb! I might have that! What about you, babe?"

"Huh?"

"Are you okay? Where's that waiter? We're ready!"

"Alicia!" said Baba, grabbing her arm. "Take me to the bathroom, please!"

"Baba, can't you go by yourself? Are you okay?" She threw a glance at me, getting up from her seat.

"You know my leg hurts. Come on!"

"Ay, Baba."

"Babe, just go be a good granddaughter and help her!"

After they left, Robert threw a glance at their direction to make sure the bathroom door had closed behind them.

"Okay, go!"

Like lightning, Leila's hand dug into her purse, pulling out a small rectangular box. She walked to the head of the table and met me there, handing it off. Robert, my mom, and Carlos kept a lookout on the bathroom door, worried it would open at any moment. I shoved the box in my jacket pocket, cold sweat running down my back.

"You sure? Last chance to back out!" said Robert, turning to me.

I could hear my blood pumping; no words came out. I nodded.

Just in time, Baba's flowered blouse turned the corner, followed by Alicia's cherry blossom romper. Baba's eyes scanned the room, and Leila's smile caused her to smile back.

"Okay!" she said, taking her seat next to me. "Now, can we eat?"

Everyone's eyes were on me. It didn't matter that I knew the answer to the question I was about to ask. All the noise in the room, the pops of champagne, the hum and laughter of people, waiters clattering about, was drowned out. My core was shaking, and everything outward followed suit. I found the right woman, and our lives were about to change forever. In this moment, all my life to now felt like a second on the clock. It was here that we stepped into the future God called us to.

I grabbed her elbow, standing up and taking her with me, praying the words would come. We locked eyes, and I was breathless.

"You know I love you. You know my heart is yours."

"Ohmygod."

I pulled the ring from my pocket, opened the box, and got down on one knee.

"Will you marry me?"

Her hands went to her mouth, looking at her mother for confirmation.

"Look down! Look *down!*" came Leila's voice.

"Ohmygod!" She started crying. Lots of crying.

My mom and Baba were laughing. And after what felt like forever. She finally nodded.

"SHE SAID YESSS!" Leila shouted.

The other tables started clapping. Everyone at ours was shouting. I got up and hugged her, soaking my shirt with tears and mascara.

"Well, put the ring on!" shouted Leila.

I don't know whose hands trembled more, hers or mine, but after three tries, I got it!

"Wrong hand, babe."

*Figures. Let's try this again.*

"It fits!" I yelled at Robert, thanking God for his girlish pinkies.

"Oh my god! Did that really just happen?" she said, wiping tears. She took a look at the ring on her hand. "Oh my god!" Looking at her dad. "So you approved it?"

Everyone started laughing. Robert hugged her tight and held her in his arms. They both cried. It took all of us for this moment to happen. It took all of us trusting in God, through bitterly painful situations, and keeping faith where none was left to keep, following Him through the dark parts of life. And He led us here.

Here He was.

They finally broke apart. Alicia finally sat down, still looking at the ring and showing it to my mom.

I turned to Leila. We were both exhausted, but beaming.

"Now we can eat!"

"Well, now I can't!" yelled Alicia. "Couldn't you have done this after dinner?"

"No!" we all yelled back.

*Glory be to God!*

# The Keeper of Promises

*Robert*

"Oh my goodness, Juvenal! God has been so good!" I sipped my water bottle. "You have no idea how many people have come up to me, neighbors, people in church, and hug me." His office was dotted with Cuban art and Star Trek memorabilia. A miniature model of the starship *Enterprise* stood on a shelf, facing a mosaic of the Cuban flag with a map of the island.

"I tell your story to my patients. Those photos you sent me, I share them, and it gives them hope," said the doctor. "The day that we told you the diagnosis, Barrios and I…you don't get it. I was crying my eyes out in the other room. It's astonishing what God has done in your life."

"I turned fifty-eight!" I laughed. "We didn't know if I would even be there to do that. They gave me until January of 2018."

"I remember. Dr. Kaywin is a good friend, and he's been excellent in keeping me updated on your progress. Those first scans, man, shesh! It's a miracle!"

"That's what Kaywin calls me now. Every time I walk into his office, he throws his hands up and yells, 'Miracle Man!' I didn't think he was a man of faith, but either way, God used him in a big, big way in my life." I leaned back. "I used to weigh 149 at my lowest. At the last weigh-in, I'm over 200! I'm getting fat, man!"

"You can eat as much as you like. I'm sure Leila won't mind."

"That's what she says as she feeds me ice cream. I tell you, I would not be here if it weren't for her faith. You hear stories of guys getting sick, like I was, and their wives leaving because it's too hard. She never did that." I felt my eyes welling up. "What a woman!"

"I've known her parents since we were teenagers. She's just like them, the best of both of them."

"And she changed through this process!" I leaned forward, resting my elbows on his desk. "Oh my goodness, Juvenal! She used to be the type to avoid confrontation and just block it out when anything bad was happening. You should have seen her fight with the insurance when they denied a scan or a medication. She was fierce!"

"And how is she doing now?"

"It's funny, in the BC—before cancer—she had an appreciation for God, but nothing like now. Her relationship with Him is totally different. Her students saw her reading the Bible before class one day and started to ask questions. After a week, a whole group of them got together before class to read and discuss the Bible. They're nine-year-olds! It's amazing."

"And you? How are you feeling now?"

I paused for a second. A tiny figurine of Captain America caught my eye, nestled between photos of his kids and his racquetball buddies.

"I'm great!" I smiled. "After a few scans, it turns out the adrenal gland had a spot of cancer on it. It wasn't inflammation. But it didn't bother me. God healed me. How we got there was up to Him."

"Radiation?" Juvenal sipped his coffee. "No chemo?"

"Just radiation. Dr. Mehta zapped it a few times and that was the end of it. Then a few months later, another spot showed up."

"I saw the scans, a lymph node close to the adrenal gland. This time, it was Dr. Kotcheka?"

"Yeah, he's a doctor on Mehta's team. They're both great. I wasn't happy about these spots showing up. Obviously, there's a little voice from the devil whispering in your ear, 'It's back!' But you know where that voice comes from and how to get rid of it quick!"

"That's important. We tell patients all the time that hope and a positive outlook are crucial in this process. Sadly, the person gives up and the body follows. You have to feed your hope."

"You know I go to DiamondHead every year, out by Ft. Myers. Because it's a times-hare, it's the same people year after year. Leila and I made friends with another couple. A few months ago, I got a call from the wife. The husband had cancer. This was in October of last year. We visited them. I shared my testimony, and we prayed together. He accepted Jesus with me. It broke my heart to hear that he passed away in February."

"Lung cancer?

"Yeah, same as me, though not quite so bad. I struggled with that. How come he died and I got healed? You know?"

"Sometimes we never get to know the answer to these questions."

"You're right. I surrendered everything to God, and I believe that He healed me, and that's how I live my life. But there were times that I was ready to go. And I would tell God, 'Take me home. I can't do this anymore.' Sometimes, that's a mercy."

"'To be absent from the body is to be present with the Lord,' right?"

"That's right!" I laughed. "The main thing is that he's with God now. And that's always going to be better than the best day here. Whether I live or die, I will praise Him, not for what He can do for me, but because He is so good!"

"Always."

"Juvenal, I want to thank you for always being there. In the early mornings, even in the middle of the night, you were always a text away, and you always had time for me. You have no idea how much peace and comfort you gave me. To have a doctor like that on your side." My voice was breaking. "You were proof of God's hand in my life."

I pulled out my phone and scrolled through his text messages.

"You sent me this while I was all skinny and sick. I don't know if you remember. 'Your weakness is an opportunity to grow strong in awareness of My Almighty presence. Go gently through this day leaning on Me and enjoying My presence. If you look back on your journey thus far, you can see days of extreme weakness have been some of your most precious times.'"

Tears rolled down my cheeks.

"I must have read that text a hundred times! Whenever I was too sick to move, I had Leila or Mauricio read it to me." I smiled, wiping my eyes. "I'm a crier now, Juvenal. Anything sets me off!"

He walked around his desk and hugged me.

"Oh! Did I tell you? We're planning a wedding!"

## Interview with Pastors

Leila was more used to makeup than I was. In the styling chair, makeup artists dabbed, brushed, and coated my face in powders.

"And what's this for?"

"To help you get not so shiny! Don't move!"

It was clear she was used to dealing with Spanish-speaking guests on the show. On the chair next to me, Leila was jabbering away with her own makeup artist in Spanish, leaving me to look like an orange on camera.

"And this?" I asked as she was dabbing an orange cream over my cheeks.

"Robert, let her do her job!" snapped Leila. "We're on in less than three minutes!"

My girl held the pad over my nose and struggled to find the words.

"Is...skin tone, yes?"

"Err...yes?"

She continued dabbing.

"Leila, I swear, if I go out on camera looking like a grapefruit..."

"Oh, relax, babe! You look fine!"

"We're ready for you now," said the production assistant that popped her head in the door.

He led us to a small studio above Alpha and Omega Church, where cameramen, audio technicians, coordinators, and teleprompters made televising a weekly TV show look like a seamless operation.

"We have the tremendous testimony of Robert Germroth, who's here with us today." We heard Delgado as we walked into the interview room, where he and his wife, Pastor Mariam, were waiting for us. "Robert had cancer, terminal cancer, and God healed him." He looked at the camera. "How did it happen? Well, pay attention to what Robert Ger-m-roth has to say!"

*Hard* G, *like* germ…*every time.*

We were seated by the time he finished the introduction. I faced him, Leila was next to me on the couch, and Pastor Mariam took an armchair by Leila. That way, they could both ask us questions and participate in the conversation without blocking the cameras.

"Now, before getting into the testimony," said Delgado, "you mentioned that you used to pass by the church and the Holy Spirit pressed on you to come here?"

"Years ago, probably like six years ago, I would drive by here on my way to Pinecrest, where most of my jobs were. The Holy Spirit kept talking to me, saying, 'You need to go to that church.' I wasn't walking with the Lord like I am now, and I even changed my commute to avoid that tugging in my spirit. But the story starts before that. My wife told me in 2010 that Joel Osteen was coming to Miami, to the American Airlines Arena. She wanted to go, so we went. You came out onstage, and immediately, the Holy Spirit went, 'You need to go to his church.'"

"Mine?" clarified Delgado. "Not Joel Osteen's?"

"Yours."

He threw his head back and laughed. A deep, hearty laugh from deep in his chest.

"I never caught your name then, and for the next two months, I asked everyone I knew." I paused. "You don't have the same body you had then. 'Who knows that heavy guy with a beard that came out onstage?' I had no idea who you were, and after a few months of asking, I forgot about it and moved on with my life. Then, around 2014, I would drive by Alpha and Omega and the Holy Spirit would talk to me. 'You need to go there.'"

"But you didn't know I was the pastor."

"Not at all. The Holy Spirit kept insisting so much that, yeah, I had to find a different route to work. I had a million excuses: 'It's a Spanish church, I won't understand anything.' 'It's a huge church, I'll just be a number there.' 'No one will know me.' But the Holy Spirit wouldn't stop. And in April 2017, I was diagnosed with lung cancer."

"You smoked?"

"Yeah. At first, they told me it wasn't a big deal, they could cut it out and I could go on with my life. You know, the pope is living with one lung. 'But let's do a PET scan first,' said the pulmonologist. I knew things were bad when my general practitioner was also in the office with the pulmonologist. The cancer was all over my body."

"At first, they thought it was just on your lung and they could cut it out."

"They just did the biopsy on the lung. Since that was where the symptoms were. But the PET scan showed cancer in my hip, a few spots in my spine, my left jaw, and two spots in my brain."

"Leila, what did you think of all this?"

"It was a very hard blow."

"You weren't expecting it?"

"It's not something you expect. In that moment, I remember I cried a lot. Just a really intense pain."

"You knew Christ already?"

"Yes…"

"He was cold in the faith, and you?"

"No. I mean, I was born Catholic. I never stepped away from Christ, I just changed churches to get closer to Him. I never felt far away. I was comfortable, and we had a relation-ship, not as much as now." She smiled. "But I always prayed and trusted in Him."

"Of course."

"I don't know if I could tell you everything that's hap-pened since the diagnosis and getting to the church, but I remember one of the first things you said about belief. It must have been one of those first Sundays that we started going. You said, 'Just believe. It's in the Bible, God said it, just believe it! End of story!' And in that moment, I told him, next to me, 'Well, Jesus says He died for you and you're healed, so that's it!'"

"What did you think, Robert? The doctor told you there's cancer all over your body. What was your mindset at that moment?"

"Fear of death. Nothing but fear."

"Fear that just wouldn't go away."

"Yes." I nodded. "Just like that. Leila immediately started a plan, you know. 'What do we do? What's the treat-ment like?' And the doctor just held up his hand, looked at me dead in the eyes, and told me, 'Mr. Germroth, there's four things you need to do if you haven't done them yet. Get your last will, your medical power of attorney, your financial power of attorney, and your living will. Then we can talk about treatment.'"

"So they were sentencing you to death, basically?" said Pastor Mariam.

"That's right," said Leila.

"The only thing missing was to tell you to prepare the funeral!" said Delgado.

"I knew what he was saying, so I said, 'Dr. Kaywin, how long do I have?' This was in May of 2017, and he told me,

'I don't like to give my patients a time frame, but let's hope you're here in January."

"Just like that?" asked Delgado. "So easily?"

"Just like that."

"I remember Robert." Pastor Mariam turned to Leila. "He was thin, *thiiiiin*, white, and with a cane. I remember him looking like that! And what God has done has been a real miracle!"

"What was the breakthrough? I want to know how you got free, how you beat Satan!" Delgado slammed his palms on the desk with each question.

"Well, after the diagnosis, we went home and I locked myself in the bathroom. I knew what I had to do. I cried my eyes out to my heavenly Father. I cried. I cried! And I begged for my life. And I didn't get peace. Then I said, 'Okay, if you're not going to give me my life, give me fifteen years, like King Hezekiah from the Bible.' So I was begging for my fifteen years and nothing. So I said, 'Okay, Lord, then just like Shadrach, Meshach, and Abednego, whether I go in the fire or I don't, whether I live one more day or a hundred more years, I will worship You, I will praise You, I will give You all the glory all the days of my life.' And immediately the peace of God fell on me and I was able to get it together and come out of that bathroom. I told my wife, who grew up Catholic—and we were going to a Lutheran church from time to time—we had to get to a spirit-filled church. One that was full of faith, that believed in God's healing, and we were starting this Sunday! I didn't know where, but we were going!

"Later on, Mauricio, my daughter's boyfriend, came to the house, and I asked him which church he went to. And he said, 'Alpha and Omega out on Miller.' I rolled my eyes, smiled, and threw my hands in the air. I get it, Lord, You want me there. I get it!"

Delgado was laughing and clapping his hands. "So that's how it happened?"

"When God wants you somewhere, He's gonna get you there!" I laughed. "So that Sunday we were there, and as soon as we got in, Pastor Mariam was in the lobby. I had my cane. Like she said, I was only 145 pounds, a huge tumor sticking out of my jaw, and she spoke to Leila. And Leila told her, 'My husband was diagnosed with lung cancer,' and she went on, 'We don't have that in this church.'"

"That's what you said, Mami?" Delgado laughed.

"I remember that! I told her, 'We are a cancer-free church!'"

"Since Leila had never been to a spirit-filled church before, I told her, 'The anointing of God only falls up to the third row.'" I laughed. "We have to sit up front! Knowing her, she would have been happy sitting at the back. But I like to be up close!"

"And there we were every Sunday, right up front," said Leila.

"God is so good! I was scared! I was afraid I would lose by breath. I hadn't been in church since the early nineties. I didn't know these new songs, but that very first song they played, it was, 'Your breath, in my lungs, so I pour out my praise to you.' That was when I knew that message was for me. And I applied it to me."

"When the doctors would tell us, 'Well, we're going to do this and that and see what happens,' you know, they had no certainty and gave us no certainty of anything. And there were patients like him who didn't have as much cancer as he did, and they would die. And some who were worse off than him still died. So we were in a situation where—"

"Where there wasn't any hope according to the world," finished Delgado.

"None," said Leila. "According to what they knew, this was terminal, and that was the end of it. But after going to church and listening to your message, Pastor, I stopped listening to the bad news the doctors told us. I would tell them, 'No, I have a heavenly Father telling me what I need to hear.' And I believed that and I wouldn't move from that. The doctor would tell me something, and my answer would always be, 'But with God there's always hope.'"

"Praise God!" said Delgado.

"Later on in the process, one of the doctors told Robert, 'Faith like hers,' so even the doctor acknowledged that it wasn't just the medicine but the faith we had that produced results."

"So this was the Word of God, used continuously like medicine, your obedience in going to church, the word received, made Rhema in you both, the revelation that God is a healer, and the power of that Word like spiritual medicine. It was a complete bombardment of the Word of God coming from all sides. I imagine this was also a testimony for the doctors," said Delgado.

"The oncologist calls him the Miracle Man."

"So I hope you told the doctor who was it that healed him—Christ Jesus!"

"Exactly!"

"Well, now," said Delgado, "God has plans with you both! This is part of that plan, you sharing what God has done with you so that others can see that if He did it with you, He can do it with them too. They just have to believe, obey, and walk in that truth."

"Without a doubt!" said Leila.

"Robert," asked Pastor Mariam, "do you have any words for those who are watching us now? Anything you'd like to tell them?"

I stopped for a second, looked in the camera facing me, spotlights blinding my eyes.

"I was not walking with God, I was not going to church when this healing started. But as I said when I was in that bathroom, I turned my whole heart, my whole soul, and my whole life over to God. Anyone who has cancer, or who has any type of disease, that's all it takes. At the same time that Jesus died on that cross and forgave your sins, He healed all your diseases. At that *same* moment it happened! In the Bible, when they lowered that lame person from the roof onto where Jesus was, He said to him, 'Your sins are forgiven. Pick up your bed and go.' The same thing He did for us. You're already healed, by what Jesus Christ did. Just surrender all to Him. It's out of His love, not out of anything that you've done, no matter where you're at right now, today. God loves you and wants to heal you. Just turn to Him. Just turn to Him and you'll be healed."

"Thank you, Leila. Thank you, Robert," said Delgado, facing the camera. "Let this testimony serve as an inspiration. If He did it for them, He can do it for you, He can do it for me, He can do it for whomever. Up to what point can you believe? Up to what point can you activate God's love in you through your faith? There are great and powerful times coming, and God wants to use you, not only to heal you, but also to use your healing as a testimony for many others. I'm still in awe of this testimony, but this is Pastor Alberto Delgado, with my wife, Mariam, signing off, reminding you that everything is possible, if you can believe!"

The show's exit melody resonated throughout the studio, echoing off the walls.

"That's a wrap!" said a production assistant.

We got up. Leila was hugging pastor Mariam goodbye. She turned to me, smiling.

"Be honest. Did I look like a grapefruit?"

Over the next few months, our attention was focused on the wedding. Leila and Alicia ran everywhere, looking for dresses, venues, poring over guest lists, and fighting about what kind of flowers would look best with the wedding colors. At first, I mistakenly thought that I would get an opinion in the process, but their murderous glares quickly cured me of that notion. Mauricio and I took refuge in work, bidding new jobs and riding around, looking for abandoned properties to rehab.

"You're lucky!" I slapped his thigh as we were sitting at a red light. "Your part is over. Until the wedding, all you have to do is shut up and show up. I have to shut up, show up, and pay up!"

He laughed. "You *get* to pay up. This is a good problem to have!"

"You're right! Can you believe it, Mauricio? Two years ago, if they had told us that this would be our life now, planning a wedding, looking for investment properties, I wouldn't have believed it. God is so, so, good!"

"What's the saying? 'He is able to do immeasurably more than all we ask or imagine.'"

"That's right, man! That's exactly right! I prayed for my healing, and he gave me that. He turned my family around to Him. He's delivered me from so much, alcohol, pot, smoking, all the things I was addicted to or held me back from Him."

## July 27

My hands were shaking outside the door. Inside, brides-maids were squealing, clattering their heels on the marble floor. Out in the distance, beyond the glass wall at the end of the hallway, the sky shone blue and bright, one of those July days that's perfect for surfing. I could see Miami Cancer Institute bathed in that summer day. Cars were pulling to the valet, delivering slowly moving shadows into the building. The skin on my thigh where the nurses accessed the port for chemo itched.

"Lord, be with those people and their families," I whispered under my breath. This process taught me that every one of them was a story. Each was a heart God was dealing with, families that held their breath, as mine did, every time an exam room opened with a doctor holding test results. Every one of them desperately needing hope, as I did.

"We're ready for you, Dad!" the photographer's assistant poke her head through the door, standing aside and holding it open for me. I saw Leila first, wearing the stunning sap-phire dress that came off the shoulders and gave her a plung-ing neckline. A corset of white roses on her wrist. I could have stood there forever, admiring every curve and detail of my wife, prettier than I had ever seen her. And before I did, I saw her, and my throat did the weird broken-vacuum thing. The line of bridesmaids in pink started laughing, dabbing their eyes to stop the tears and keep their makeup intact.

Light from the windows in the presidential suite of the hotel bounced off her nine-foot dress, filling the ceiling and the walls with a soft glow. She was resplendent. The daughter that wouldn't walk Disney but had to get in the stroller, who always had more attitude than size, stood in front of me, transformed. No longer my child, but a bride, bouquet in hand, same flowers as Leila's corset, smiling, wondering if I liked the dress, holding back tears.

"Well, Spapi?" she asked.

"Oh my goodness!" I held her tight. "My little Coosie is a bride!"

"Do you like it?"

"I've never seen a more beautiful bride!"

"Awwws" from the bridesmaids were interrupted by Leila. "Hey! What the heck, man? I married you!"

"She's beautiful!" I yelled back, keeping my eyes on my daughter.

"Yes, she is!" cooed her mother. "Maury is going to fall in love with her all over again!"

"Okay, Dad," said the photographer, "pull her in close for a hug. That's good!"

I whispered in her ear, "Just say the word and you and I are running away. I'm not ready to give up my Coosie to the monster!"

We spent the early part of the afternoon taking more photos. I barely noticed the photographer, lost instead in the details my wife and daughter showed—a curl of hair in just the right light, Leila's eyes lit up by the light bouncing off Alicia's dress, smile lines curling around their eyes as they laughed. All was beautiful, and I loved every second of it. God is so good! After the photographer was satisfied, Leila and the bridesmaids left for the church. Mauricio was already there, welcoming guests, and the girls were going to get ready for the bride's arrival.

By the time we arrived at the church, everyone had already gone inside, except for the bridal party. I could see Mauricio and Carlos, his best man, waiting at the end of the aisle for the procession to start. The groomsmen paired up with their bridesmaids, and after a nod from Leila, the music started.

The grandparents started the procession, and it was like a dam—once broken, there was no stopping it. And with each passing couple—Leila went in with her brother Peter, Mauricio's brother Enmanuel with Valerie—I felt the last seconds of my life with my daughter come to a close. After today, she would be his first, then mine. My son Robbie and his girlfriend, Nicole. It was bittersweet, like closing the door to Narnia, something that needed to happen, but nonetheless, you felt the weight of it. Chris and Lorena. Glory be to God. The maid of honor, Danielle. Time's up!

Guitar instrumentals played as we walked. We walked under a cherry blossom archway Mauricio's mom designed and we put together last night. Guests rose to their feet. Some were holding back tears; others were beaming, barely containing their cheer. As we walked, I saw many familiar faces: my siblings and their families from South Carolina, Leila's family, and many that came from Mauricio's side. Even though we did not all know one another, we were all there at that moment, and love brought us together.

Now Mauricio's hands were shaking. I sympathized with the poor kid. All of us saw Alicia pick out her dress, get ready, her makeup. For a year and a half, she would show everyone her dress, except him. She wouldn't let him see it until now. And it hit him like a freight train.

How amazing was God that weeks before I got sick, he brought me this kid! Who stopped his life, moved into my house, and took care of me when I couldn't. How amazing was God that my daughter gave her life to Christ the day after she got engaged! How indescribable is that God that let me walk my daughter down the aisle when my first thought after getting diagnosed was, 'Who will walk her when she gets married?'

We got to the end of the aisle. Not letting go of her hand, I kissed him on the cheek. Then I kissed her. I entwined their hands together, and they only had eyes for each other. I walked over to my wife, and the empty seat next to her. If God hadn't intervened when He did, that seat would still have been empty.

There were many words spoken over my life through this whole process. At first, words of death and destruction, where I would not live to see this day. Then, words of faith, calling me to stand on a reality that was not my own, until God made it my own. And finally, words of gratitude—thanks for the road we traveled. Because He was true to His promise, and out of our despair, he turned it to good. Now in my life in Christ, and in any situation where words are spoken, I know this: God has the final word.

I kissed my wife and held her hand tight. Pastor Pedro was starting.

"Weddings are a new beginning…"

# Postscript

Robert passed away on October 15, 2020, from neoplastic meningitis.

There are no words to describe the confusion and maelstrom of emotions that our family went through in the weeks prior to his passing, or the weeks since. And in that time, we questioned *everything*. And God, in His grace, was preparing to teach us a severe mercy—this world is not the destination.

Chapter 9 ends with our wedding. Throughout that year and the next, Robert thrived, healthy, sharing his testimony with everyone who would hear it—this included hounding me to write this book. "The Holy Spirit told me you're the man to write this book," he would say. "I believe that this is going to bless so many people and point them toward God." I thought he was crazy, but I was crazy enough to go along with it, and here we are *fifty-seven thousand words* later! After his passing, I wrestled with the decision whether to add this postscript or leave the ending as it was. After all, what do you do with a healing testimony when the patient dies? It felt like a cruel joke was played on us.

But God, in His mercy, reminded me of the title—He has the final word. And even in all this, even in the whole story, He deserves to be trusted. So we hide nothing—this has been our story, and this is what God has done in our lives; in mercy to us, for his Glory, and that you may know Him, and trust Him in your need.

At the end of December 2019, his voice changed. None of the doctors could figure out why, but something was pressing a nerve in his brain that made it difficult for him to speak as he did. This meant going back to the cancer center for scans and tests which yielded no answers. Then 2020 happened, and in the midst of a global pandemic, doctors were concerned that cancer cells showed up in the spinal fluid and recommended a full brain radiation and chemotherapy. While debating whether to go along with treatment, the Holy Spirit took him several times to Galatians 2:20 (NKJV):

> I have been crucified with Christ; it is no longer I who live, but Christ lives in me; and the *life* which I now live in the flesh I live by faith in the Son of God, who loved me and gave Himself for me.

We did not understand those words at the time, at least not as deeply as we've come to know them since. For the rest of that year, through ten straight days of full brain radiation and chemotherapy, Robert was slowly losing attachments to the world. Because of his tongue and weakness from the chemotherapy, there were no more Bible study groups at home. Then COVID-19 cemented that with months of quarantine and isolation, where his world was even more reduced to just his wife, Leila, and video chatting with family and members of the church.

In the months that followed, he delegated responsibilities in his work and his only interest was the Word of God. "I feel such at peace about everything, Mauricio. I can't explain it. I'm not worried about the jobs, about my health, my finances, nothing. All I know is that people are going to see the glory of God manifest. But I'm done with this, man.

I'm tired of hospitals, doctors, and tests," he would tell me. And I didn't know what to make of that.

His physical condition weakened, developing thrush and making it difficult to eat solid food. Again, he got skinny then emaciated. He started sleeping more and there were fights to even drink nutrients. Leila would ask him, "Are you going to have an Ensure for dinner?" With a sigh, "If you want me to" came his reply. "But don't be disappointed if I can't drink it."

These were very hard times because while Robert was losing interest in the world, Leila was fighting even harder to keep him going. Eventually, he started losing strength in one leg, causing him to use a cane. By next Sunday, both legs had gone, and he was in a wheelchair at church. The Sunday after that, his energy was so low, he fell asleep during church.

He passed away the next Thursday.

His condition deteriorated so much, so rapidly that he needed constant care around the clock. We paid for nurses and caretakers to sit with him when we couldn't, and his son, Robbie, and I took the afternoons to give Leila time to get home from work, shower, and take over. Until eventually, even that became too much. He was in constant pain and couldn't move by himself, so he needed to be repositioned every ten minutes to relieve the pressure on his hips or spine.

I moved back in with him and Leila to help during the nights. And I'll tell you, it's easy to ask God "why are we going through this and where are You and when are You going to do something about this" when you've gotten up thirteen times a night to help him get comfortable and you haven't slept in three days and you have another hard day of work in a few hours. It's easy to resent the situation you're in at that moment and try to take it out on God, but God was right there. We felt His presence, and He was the one to see us through this.

In the weeks after, when we were trying to process this, Leila would say, "How in the heck was I able to lift him and move him and just *function*?" We did not appreciate it fully at the time, but God walked us through this situation. He closed all the doors and windows so we wouldn't run away, and then He held our hands as we went through the unimaginable.

That Thursday morning, Leila went to work as she normally did, Alicia was in Jacksonville, Florida, at a new job, and I was supposed to leave for the jobsite in the morning. The nurse that was with him the night before said he was uncomfortable all night, and she looked exhausted. I could tell that she had been repositioning him all night, and he finally fell asleep around five in the morning. At seven in the morning, the replacement nurse that came in only spoke Spanish, which was a problem since there would be no one home to translate for Robert. That same nurse requested an English-speaking replacement and generously offered to stay and help until they found one. I stayed too to translate.

By 8 a.m., Robert hadn't woken up, and the nurses were unsure if it was due to medication or something else. When I updated Leila and Alicia, both asked if they should go home. For some reason, I said yes. It couldn't hurt to spend more time with him. After I hung up with the girls, he woke up for a minute, asked for them, and I told him they're on their way. Before he closed his eyes, I said, "I love you, Rob." He smiled and closed his eyes. "I love you too," he said and went back to sleep.

The replacement nurse showed up around 9 a.m. and Leila around at the same time. Alicia started the four hundred-mile trip down. His breathing then became labored and was taking thirty-six breaths per minute—the normal is between twelve and twenty. Breathing that much meant that the heart was overcompensating and, if it continued, he could suffer a heart attack.

Robbie was helping a friend move. I called him, and he came over with his fiancée. Leila's parents also came over. No one said he was dying, yet everyone felt the same pull to be there.

As the hours passed, Leila spent the time stroking his arm, whispering how much she loved him. I called Alicia every twenty minutes to see how close she was. By 2 p.m., his skin color turned grey, and he started gasping for air—even though he was on constant oxygen set at max. Nurses kept giving him morphine every hour to numb his pain and keep him comfortable. And all the while, I was praying that Alicia would make it. If he passed and she missed it, it would be a wound that she would carry for the rest of her life. At 2:20 p.m., his gasps became slower and slower. The nurse lifted his shirt above the navel to show us his pulse. At 2:25 p.m., Robbie opened the house door, with Alicia on the phone, and he was yelling, "Don't turn off the car, park on the grass, and just RUN!"

She rushed in to his bed in the living room, still in her bright blue scrubs from work, threw herself on his chest. "Spapi, I'm here. Spapi, wake up. I'm here, I made it!" She felt his chest rise one last time, and he was gone. In the middle of our world crumbling, God answered my prayer. She got there seconds before he passed, and God held him there for her.

In the days that followed, in his memorial service, hundreds of people came to pay their respects. And in the same chapel where fifteen months before Alicia and I celebrated our happiest day, we were also saying goodbye to a father to us both. And Pastor Pedro, the same pastor who married us, held us through the memorial service. "Robert loved big, and he served the Lord with all his heart," he said. "And I know he would have wanted, even now, the opportunity for those who do not know Christ to do so, so they can see the same God that Robert is now seeing in splendor."

Seven people gave their lives to Christ that day.

This isn't a story of a miraculous healing, even though there was one. This is the story of people who trust God, not for the happy ending, but because He is worthy of that trust. Because He has proven time and time again that we do not serve Him because of what He can do for us, but because He loved us first and gave all of Himself to have that relationship with us. This is a story of people who trusted God and God transformed them. The story is not over, and your story is not over, and no matter what you're going through, remember that God *has the final word.*

# Bible Scriptures

What the Word of God says in times of trouble.

Heal me, O Lord, and I will be healed; save me and I will be saved, for you are the one I praise. (Jer. 17:14)

If you listen carefully to the LORD your God and do what is right in his eyes, if you pay attention to his commands and keep all his decrees, I will not bring on you any of the diseases I brought on the Egyptians, for I am the LORD, who heals you. (Exod. 15:26)

So do not fear, for I am with you; do not be dismayed, for I am your God. I will strengthen you and help you; I will uphold you with my righteous right hand. (Isa. 41:10)

Surely he took up our pain and bore our suffering, yet we considered him punished by God, stricken by him, and afflicted. But he was pierced for our transgressions, he was crushed for our iniquities; the punishment that brought us peace was on him, and by his wounds we are healed. (Isa. 53:4–5)

"But I will restore you to health and heal your wounds," declares the LORD. (Jer. 30:17)

You restored me to health and let me live. Surely it was for my benefit that I suffered such anguish. In your love you kept me from the pit of destruction; you have put all my sins behind your back. (Isa. 38:16–17)

And my God will meet all your needs according to the riches of his glory in Christ Jesus. (Phil. 4:19)

Then they cried to the LORD in their trouble, and he saved them from their distress. He sent out his word and healed them; he rescued them from the grave. Let them give thanks to the LORD for his unfailing love and his wonderful deeds for mankind. (Ps. 107:19–21)

LORD my God, I called to you for help, and you healed Me. (Ps. 30:2)

He will make an utter end of it: affliction shall not rise up a second time. (Nah. 1:9)

Therefore I tell you, whatever you ask for in prayer, believe that you have received it, and it will be yours. (Mark 11:22–24)

I shall not die, but live, and declare the works of the Lord. (Ps. 118:17 NKJV)

Fear not, for I *am* with you; Be not dismayed, for I *am* your God. I will strengthen you, Yes, I will help you, I will uphold you with My righteous right hand. (Isa. 41:10 NKJV)

God the Refuge of His People and Conqueror of the Nations. (Ps. 46:1)

God *is* our refuge and strength, [a] very present help in trouble.

For I know the thoughts that I think toward you, says the Lord, thoughts of peace and not of evil, to give you a future and a hope. (Jer. 29:11 NKJV)

Blessed *are* the merciful, For they shall obtain mercy. (Matt. 5:7 NKJV)

The Lord *is* good, A stronghold in the day of trouble; And He knows those who trust in Him. (Nah. 1:7 NKJV)

Bonus

# Introduction

*Tuesday, January 26, 2021*

I wrote this book out of the conversations I shared with loved ones having just lost my father-in-law. While we felt the raw emotions of dealing with his absence, we wondered, *Where is God in all this?* Didn't we do everything asked of us? We went to church, we tithed faithfully, we gathered together at home to worship, and we shared Jesus with others everywhere we went, so what gives?

In those conversations with my mother-in-law, she and I examined the past few months of his decline, his sudden death, and the shock of a reality without the most dynamic man our family knew. Where we had seen cancer come and go in our lives and seen God manifest, in a big way, how were we to interpret this staggering blow that shook everything?

The conclusion was a hard truth—God does not spare you pain. He did not spare His own son, and He did everything right. Sometimes, doing things right will take us through pain and loss that we cannot avoid. Nowhere in the Bible does God promise a life free from pain, but He does promise to be with us as we go through it.

We noticed that in the numbness of those days, when the weight of his absence was fresh in our minds, we felt God the most too. His presence and His revelation into why we go through pain and why He allows this is why I wrote this book. Life can be wonderful, but it has a savagery to it that can destroy things we've worked decades to grow and protect. Sometimes, that loss is a mercy from God in an excruciating disguise. Sometimes, coming to these conclusions takes years of suffering. It is my prayer that what you find in this book helps shorten the time to your healing.

Time does not heal. God does.

These are the savage mercies.

# The Savage Mercies

There is a truth that ties us all together; we are not sheltered from pain. It is the inescapable truth we all must face many, many times over. You have lost someone and your world has crashed down around you, or you've failed to hold on to something you wanted. The end is the same—you know the pain a crisis brings.

And God *allowed* it.

In my life, God allowed my parent's divorce and allowed my brother and I to grow up without a father. He allowed financial instability to plague us as we were growing up. I remember the three of us sleeping in a basement that flooded every night, waking up to four inches of water in the mornings because we had nowhere else to stay.

And God *allowed* it.

I know what it's like to be in several wrong relationships that destroy more than they build and not knowing how to get what I truly want from them—to go through painful breakups and see potential futures come crashing down.

I know what it's like to be a foreigner in a different country and start from square one. *Twice*.

I know what it's like to love someone going through cancer. I know what it's like to lose them.

And God *allowed* it. All of it.

I know crisis. I know what it's like to see it coming, and you can't escape it. Be in one. And finally, go through it on the other side. And I am not the only one.

The point is: man goes through pain and God allows it. Why? *Why do terrible things happen to good people?*

I've heard all my life that you shouldn't question God and that "His ways are higher than our ways" and we should trust His wisdom. Which is true...to a point. But I believe that robs us of the opportunity to know Him. After all, if we go through the terrible things, might as well get something out of it.

So with that intention, why do terrible things happen to good people? To understand that question, it needs to be broken down:

*Terrible things.* Just because something bad happens to you, does not mean that it's a terrible thing. A scalpel can take away life as well as save it. It all depends of who is at the other end of it. Sometimes a bone that healed wrong must be broken to mend correctly. Likewise, just because you go through something terrible, does not mean that it's a terrible thing in itself. It can be just the thing you need at the time.

*Good people.* How do you define *good*? While there are many arguments, let's be honest. God is good. None of us are. Not really and not for long.

So the way the question is framed implies that a person is undeserving of whatever bad thing is happening to them. It's like you're standing on a field and a meteorite just happened to fall on your head. This is a legalistic way of asking it, but it ignores context. It ignores where you've been, where you are going, who you are, and how you change. It also ignores *who* is sending the meteorite. Sometimes it's God... sometimes it's you.

A better way to frame this question is to look at it this way: your life has a beginning, it has an end, and you have an eternal destination. As you go through this life, you have a set of purposes God designed just for you (whether you do them or not—the instructions are for you), and there will be things (distractions, misinformation, crises) that will try to derail you from it and keep you where you are comfortable.

*None of God's purposes for your life are in a comfort zone.* So God sends meteorites to break what needs to be broken *in you.* And the crises do their work in correcting your focus, taking away distractions that would be destructive to you, and they change the trajectory of your life.

So instead of saying that terrible things happen to good people, it's better to say that we are all patients in the same hospital requiring different treatments from the same physician.

## God Has the Final Word

When I wrote *God Has the Final Word,* I knew that one of the purposes of my life was to show love and serve my father-in-law, Robert. I loved that man with everything I had in me. For three years, I took him to most medical appointments, helped him run his business from the hospital, and I saw how God changed us and healed him of stage 4 lung cancer.

I saw a good man with a hidden weakness (smoking three packs of cigarettes a day) being thrown into the biggest crisis of his life and his family's. The weakness he hid for years from his wife and daughter was now on full display for the world to see. In that crisis, his world ended. God transformed him from a man who changed his routine to avoid a certain church to going there every Sunday. The crisis brought him, his wife, and his daughter closer to God and closer to each other. He surrendered everything to God, and everywhere he went during the crisis, he glorified God with everything he had, even before being healed.

When he passed away, we struggled with understanding. We did everything God instructed us to; why did he still die? I would be lying if I said that we don't wrestle with that still, but since his passing, God has shown us that there is a purpose for that too and that He makes good come even from this.

This is the lesson that inspired this book—even when you do everything right, you may still not get what you want. Sometimes what we need most is what we least want. It is a hard thing to say to his widow that maybe her husband needed to be gone so her relationship with God would take center stage. It's a harder thing to go through it. Hardest still that it's true.

These are the savage mercies—that God allows suffering, pain, disappointment, and dejection in our lives because in the end, they conform to His purposes. He uses pain to remove any obstacle, building any bridge, and transforming you so there is a perfect reconciliation between you and Him. That He might, in all things, show you the infinite love you were created to receive and become the person equipped to love and receive in kind. Everything else is subject to interpretation, but this is the cornerstone of God's interaction with mankind.

> [God] is not wearied by our sins, or our indifference; and, therefore, it is quite relentless in its determination that we shall be cured of those sins, at whatever cost to us, at whatever cost to Him. (C. S. Lewis)

## *On Sins*

In the very long and very oversimplified way of looking at it, *sin* is anything that you put in front of God. Anything that separates you from Him. Anything that occupies the place He has chosen to claim over your life. Anything that takes you out of alignment with Him.

The moral law given in the Bible is actually an act of grace. It is the first lesson in how to behave in relation to Him and to others. God knew that alone we'd never get it, and we would never even be aware of our sins or how to reconcile with Him. So He started interacting with the human race in the way we could understand, and He held himself back, speaking through judges, kings, and prophets because we were not ready to receive His undiluted voice.

When Jesus comes, He fulfills the law. By His mission, He reconciles mankind to the Father. By bringing the Holy Spirit, we become changed and can interact with the Father as Jesus does.

> On that day you will realize that I am in
> my Father, and you are in me, and I am
> in you. (John 14:20)

That fulfillment of the law only means that there is a new and more efficient way to commune with the Father. Where before, we did it through a proxy; now we do it ourselves, organically, like the difference between a person that follows a recipe to make a pie and a baker that that has done so many pies that he knows how to do them all. Spiritually, the law is the foundation, but the new covenant goes a step beyond—*everything brings you closer to Him.* He raised the standard for how we should interact with Him. This kind of spiritual interfusion is precisely what God came to expect of us. Once we get to that point, the real work on our spirit begins.

## The Nature of Man

Ever since the garden of Eden, man has developed an awareness of his imperfection and an instinct for self-preservation.

> But the LORD God called out to the man,
> "Where are you?"
> "I heard Your voice in the garden,"
> he replied, "and I was afraid because I
> was naked; so I hid myself." (Gen. 3:10)

In that one line of scripture, the essence of our human nature is summarized. We are aware of our flaws, but instead of bringing them to light, we hide. This is the hole that we create for ourselves and the trap that sin creates in us. Adam said these words after doing the one thing God told him not to do. There was no moral law at that time. Before sin came into the picture, there was no division between him and God. In choosing to eat of the fruit of the tree of knowledge of good and evil, he chose something *above* the command that God gave him. He obeyed something other than God and created the first separation between them. That separation is sin.

That same nature follows us. We all have areas that we keep separate from God. We are weak. We don't like change thrown on us. We don't like diets. We love our comfort zones. We don't like confrontation. We hide and try to avoid discomfort and change. All of these statements speak the condition of a creature that is perfectly happy seeking its own comforts and satisfying its own desires, who has no interest in being interfered with and any outside influence is met with distrust and a healthy degree of hiding.

So any intervention, we call it a crisis. But God knows that if left untreated, these very areas will cause our destruction. Remember this, God must be first in *all things*. He goes first, He decides our lives, and we hold on to nothing harder than we hold on to Him. Doing anything else is putting Him in second place. We are so rooted to holding on to the areas of our comfort that any change we interpret as a crisis.

For this reason, Jesus said:

> Whoever wants to save their life will lose
> it, but whoever loses their life for me will
> save it. (Luke 9:24)

Anything that separates any part of you from God will eventually be something that will either have to be surrendered or cut away. God will not have it any other way. He calls us to Himself so we may be filled with Him and Him alone, and everything else is secondary.

The wages of sin are death. Death is a separation between the spirit and the body, between man and God, but more like an amputation because you are being cut off from the source of life. Jesus came that we might have life and life in abundance. Life comes from God. To bring life to what was dead is more like a surgical reattachment than anything else. And sometimes, that takes a crisis. What we interpret as our world falling apart on us is sometimes God performing surgery to save us from something eternally worse.

## *The Nature of God*

We tend to live in this dichotomy: God loves us and wants the best for us, yet when the crisis comes, He's nowhere to be found. If He is good, why does He allow pain? If He is all powerful, why doesn't He do something about it? The truth is that not even God is immune to pain. This is not a commentary on His limitations, for He has none, but on His humility.

A deep truth is hinged on this perspective: we see pain as something to avoid. He allows Himself to feel pain in order to connect with us. No one is spared from pain. Not us. Not Him. Not even Jesus.

> My Father, if it is possible, may this cup
> be taken from me. Yet not as I will, but as
> you will. (Matt. 26:39)

God never allows us to go through something He is not willing to go through Himself. He is not absent in our sufferings. Whether we perceive Him or not does not change that fact. There have been times when I have not felt God's presence in my time of pain, when I knock at the door of heaven and find it closed. And it's easy to feel even more alone and abandoned then, but God presents Himself in other ways to me at those moments. Either through a person He's assigned to me or a message that hits home at just the right time or some other way entirely. Looking for God at those times of crisis is sometimes looking for comfort and reassurance, and sometimes He denies it because He means you to act. He prescribes discomfort now to make you move toward something He means for you to focus on.

He never left your side, and He never abandoned you, but He will change circumstances around you and within you to get you to act.

There are a few things to note, and I'll go further into them in the upcoming chapters:

*God is love.* That does not change. In every part of the Bible, God has shown His love for people. His very character is love. Love just means more and is deeper than what you and I know as love.

*God does not lose.* In every battle, He wins. He does not like losing; it's not in His nature. But there are battlefields that He has chosen not to engage in directly.

*He does not go against His word.* He does not violate our free will. We always have a choice in every matter. He never takes the element of choice away from us. At any point, we can chose *Him* or choose *away* from Him.

*He chooses to act* through *people.* He raises people that have gone through their own processes to help others going through their processes to come to Him. In the world, He has always acted through someone—prophets, judges, ministers, and even His own son. He acts with just enough restraint that you may come closer without overwhelming you. And He uses people to show you what can happen when someone gives their lives to Him and what He can do with them.

*He will not spare you pain.* There are avoidable pains. There are pains He protects you from. But there are others that He will not, those He will use to work something with you. He does this for many purposes, but one is this: it makes you sensitive to someone else that is going or will go through it, like a wife who experienced the loss of her husband reacts to another person that just lost a loved one. It's the gravity of the phrase: *"I do know what you are going through."* Until your character gets more like His, pain is a tool to make you aware that someone else is suffering and unlocks within you the action to help, as God have you act.

He does not pity you. He loves you too much to pity you.

> He does not respond to your pain but to your pursuit of Him. (Mike Murdock, *1001 Wisdom Keys*)

*He gave all of Himself for us and expects the same.* In the sacrifice of Jesus, He gave all of Himself for us. He spared Himself nothing and suffered the abuse of whom He most cherished. Because He loved us to that degree, when we were unlovable, He has the right to expect the same of us. Because He loved us without reservation, He has gained the right to expect it of us. So that we might love Him and He might love us without obstacle and without reservation—a love that gave all and receives all.

## How God Sees Man

Who we are, at any point in our lives, is not hidden from God. The focus of God is the heart. The same God that says that we were made in His image (Gen. 1:26) also says that the "heart is deceitful above all things, and desperately sick" (Jer. 17:19). At first glance, it's easy to assume that the statements are contradictory. After all, if we were made in the image of God and our hearts are deceitful, does that mean His is too?

No. Not in the slightest.

God, being outside of time, sees us at the same time as who we were, who we now are, and who we are going to be. If you ever have the time, do this. Fill a glass with water from the sink. Hold it up and then pour the water back slowly into the sink. You'll notice that the water hits the sink while still being inside the glass. The water is in three places at once; it is constrained by the glass in one end, suspended in transit, and splattering freely at the other end—simultaneously. In that moment, two things are true at once: the water is contained and free. The final state of it will be determined after it run its course.

God's statements on the human heart, though appearing contradictory, are actually true across a progression of time. Like the water, the heart fluctuates. There are areas that need more work than others, there are hearts that are yet unredeemed, and the final state of the heart will be determined at the moment the person dies—when there are no more decisions to make. God works on live hearts on those that are willing to let Him.

*He knows we need help...*

Whether we know it or not, sin has done a number on our hearts. We hide, we lie, and we deny. We are willing to do anything so the ugly parts of us are not exposed, brought to light, and examined by someone else. Given that trajectory, it's not hard to imagine where hearts like that go.

> The Lord saw that the wickedness of man was great in the earth, and that every intention of the thoughts of his heart was only evil continually. (Gen. 6:5)

> The heart is deceitful above all things, and desperately sick; who can understand it? (Jer. 17:9)

> For out of the heart come evil thoughts, murder, adultery, sexual immorality,

theft, false witness, slander. These are what defile a person. (Matt. 15:18)

You have neither part nor lot in this matter, for your heart is not right before God. (Acts 8:21)

He made us in His image. We have a heart because He has one. We love because He loves us, and He designed our hearts to be aligned with His. Any deviation brings out a corruption that spreads through the spirit and the body. It doesn't happen all at once, but continually, gradually, this corruption does happen, and the worse the disease is, the more aggressive the treatment.

That corruption is so gentle that you don't notice how far off course it's taken you until it's too late. The same way a married man may have impure thoughts about another woman and continues to have them until the thoughts themselves don't satisfy. Then he may flirt, but only "innocently" with that woman until that runs its course, and they find themselves alone sharing a kiss he will regret and tell himself "it's the last time." But if true repentance doesn't happen, he will continue seeing the other woman and destroy his marriage.

They are darkened in their understanding, alienated from the life of God because of the ignorance that is in them, due to their hardness of heart. (Eph. 4:18)

Every way of a man is right in his own eyes, but the Lord weighs the heart. (Prov. 21:12)

We are so used to our sins and our nature and the way things have always been done that we have no idea, except in rare glimpses, just how *good* "good" is supposed to be. We cannot come by it through our own conclusions. We cannot generate it from ourselves without God. It comes from Him, and until He shows us, we won't really recognize it. Even more so, what we think as good, when held up to the standard of God, is just another abomination.

> And he said to them, "You are those who justify yourselves before men, but God knows your hearts. For what is exalted among men is an abomination in the sight of God." (Luke 16:15)

We would have been, as the Bible says, "dead in our sins" (Eph. 2:1). We separate from God but still stuck with our sins, continuing to corrupt our nature.

*He knows we need help...because we cannot help ourselves.*

If He had not intervened, all of our hearts would be destined for the fire. If that corruption ran its course unchecked, every year, we would become worse and more abominable versions of ourselves, suffering that corruption to change our nature and our perspectives. But thank God He did!

> You will seek me and find me, when you seek me with all your heart. (Jer. 29:13)

He did not just intervene to save us from hell. That's not how it works. The grace of the sacrifice of Jesus is that at any moment, anyone with a believing and honest heart can cry out to God, and God will answer. That is His love. But for those that have years ahead of their death, that surrender their hearts to Christ, they are saved—but the work of *undoing* the generations of corruption is only beginning.

Now that you gave God access to your heart, He will dwell in it, as you asked Him to and as you need Him. But know that He does not dwell with corruption without changing it. It's His nature. The same way it's my mother-in-law's nature to pick up a broom when she sees a breadcrumb on the floor. He can't help it. Whatever He is allowed to encounter, He will transform, but always with your permission.

People get stuck in this section of the view, believing that God so focuses on your sins that He is indifferent to everything else. But the truth is that there is far more to see! You see your sin and the struggles and think that's all there is to Christianity. But in reality, it's in those struggles that the Lord of eternity is working on you, polishing what needs to be polished, breaking the twisted limbs to set them right again, and cutting open festering wounds to scoop out the rot and heal them once and for all.

The struggles that you are feeling now are simply ones that we all have gone through. We're all patients in the same hospital, being cared for by the same physician. We may be getting different treatments, but it's the same doctor.

## He Who Has Ears to Hear

There are several times in the Bible where Jesus said, "He who has ears, let him hear," and it always struck me as an odd phrase. I mean, even people who had an ear cut off could hear, and there were people with both ears who were deaf. But in this context, those words might carry a deeper meaning.

When you are knowing God and He is working in you, first, He has you know Him more. You will learn to recognize

His character, His Holiness, the sweetness of His spirit. Then there are times when all of that is shut off—completely. But maybe God allows that to develop your spiritual ears and eyes and tongue and hands.

Maybe some challenges in life, God schedules them to develop a particular spiritual area in your life, and the pain of that does not compare to the joy that new spiritual organ brings.

After all, puberty was pretty traumatic: hair in all the weird places, pimples, growing pains from bones lengthening, but without all of that, you would not be who you are today. You would not have been equipped to handle the responsibilities and joys that are yours today.

The point is that the Lord of eternity, sitting at the end of all things, can spot you out from the crowd of all the billions of people that came before you and will come behind you. He knows you, knows what you need, and knows how to reach you. And He knows how to develop you into what He has in mind. You are not lost to God, and the trials you're going through now are Him reaching you in the only way that you'll respond as you need to.

He does most of the heavy lifting. All He asks is your permission to transform you, your trust in what He's doing in your life, and your obedience to His instructions. He really handles the rest.

> Do not be conformed to this world, but
> be transformed by the renewal of your
> mind, that by testing you may discern
> what is the will of God, what is good and
> acceptable and perfect. (Rom. 12:2)

> And I will give them one heart, and a
> new spirit I will put within them. I will
> remove the heart of stone from their flesh
> and give them a heart of flesh, that they
> may walk in my statutes and keep my
> rules and obey them. And they shall be
> my people, and I will be their God. But
> as for those whose heart goes after their
> detestable things and their abominations,
> I will bring their deeds upon their own
> heads, declares the Lord God. (Ezek.
> 11:19–21)

The promises of God are conditional. When dealing
with a crisis, or in the aftermath of one, when we're looking
at the broken pieces of our world and figuring out how to put
them back together, it's easy to feel anger at God. After all,
being a Christian, we hold on to the promises that God has
in His word, and we draw comfort from them.

After all, the Bible reminds us that:

> You will keep in perfect peace those
> whose minds are steadfast, because they
> trust in you. (Isa. 26:13)

> "For I know the plans I have for you,"
> declares the LORD, "plans to prosper you
> and not to harm you, plans to give you
> hope and a future." (Jer. 29:11)

> Surely he will save you from the fowler's
> snare and from the deadly pestilence. (Ps.
> 91:3)

And we know that in all things God works for the good of those who love him, who have been called according to his purpose. (Rom. 8:28)

"No weapon forged against you will prevail, and you will refute every tongue that accuses you. This is the heritage of the servants of the LORD, and this is their vindication from me," declares the LORD. (Isa. 54:17)

Therefore I tell you, whatever you ask for in prayer, believe that you have received it, and it will be yours. (Mark: 11:24)

And my God will meet all your needs according to the riches of his glory in Christ Jesus. (Phil. 4:19)

The righteous cry out, and the LORD hears them; he delivers them from all their troubles. (Ps. 34:17)

Take delight in the LORD, and he will give you the desires of your heart. (Ps. 37:4)

Is anyone among you sick? Let them call the elders of the church to pray over them and anoint them with oil in the name of the Lord. And the prayer offered in faith will make the sick person well; the Lord

> will raise them up. If they have sinned,
> they will be forgiven. (James 5:14–15)

I've been there many times, reading words of hope and comfort and finding them bitterly ironic. Where were the promises when we were praying for a dying relative? Where was God meeting all my needs when I had no money to pay my bills?

It's hard to reconcile a broken life with a God that promises restoration, protection, and provision. It's one thing to be down in life and then hear about God when you're in the hole and someone throws you a lifeline. It's another thing to be walking with God for years and still find yourself in the midst of these circumstances.

That's when you think, *I thought I was doing everything right. I was tithing, praying, sacrificing, and worshipping. Why the hell am I still finding myself in these situations? If I prayed and believed that my father-in-law would be healed, if I laid hands and not wavered, why did he still die? Lord, didn't you promise?*

These are the hard questions to ask God. If He is love—all the time—and if He is a father—our Father—why do the promises He suggested not happen in our lives? Why does life go diametrically opposed to what He promises sometimes, especially when we need it the most?

And I believe, to answer that, we have to take several things into account:

• Do we want the promises more than we want Him?

The whole of scripture rests on this foundation: *how we react to God determines what He does next.* When we confess our sins and recognize that Jesus is the one who died for them and is raised again, we become *saved*. When we seek Him with all our heart, we find Him. When we ignore His laws and His commandments, we do so at our destruction. Our actions have divine consequences.

So when we go through trials and problems and catastrophes, how do we react? Sometimes we expect God to keep us in happy circumstances because we do the right thing. But that is short-lived. His grace allows that so you may know Him more, but the moment you get comfortable with things in your life while ignoring Him, then He will withdraw those good things. The question He presents to us is *"Do you love Me for Me or for what I provide?"*

And if the answer isn't the right one, we have work to do.

Remember, God comes first, and even when you complete everything that He requires of you, He still wants a daily relationship with you. And even when the good things are taken away, He expects you to trust Him and show Him that we are in this no matter what. No matter the good and the bad, our love for Him matches His love for us and does not waver.

I told you, He wants to love you infinitely and wants to be loved the same way. There is no second place.

- The promises are there to show you the kingdom of heaven.

  Our Father in heaven, hallowed be your name, your kingdom come, your will be done, on earth as it is in heaven. (Matt. 6:9–13)

God purposely allows us to know how things are supposed to be. The kingdom of heaven is a system of government where God is in charge. This is a system where everything aligns to the will of the Father, in perfect harmony, where good things happen, at the right time and in the right way for the intended benefit of the recipient, where everything is *perfect*—to God's definition of the word.

Humanity, as a whole, does not live in the kingdom of heaven. Ever since the garden of Eden, where God gave mankind free will, He has also allowed for us to rule ourselves. In His restraint, He would not let the authority of heaven, no matter how good it is, to impose on the authority of mankind. For mankind to receive the kingdom of heaven, it would have to willingly ask for it.

Throughout the Old Testament, God has sent mankind people that carry His message glimpses of how things can be when submitted to God. The promises of God showed His people the character of God, His faithfulness, His unwillingness to tolerate iniquity, and the rewards for obedience. Throughout the generations and through many trials, tests, and enemies, God showed His people just *who* He is to them; and by showing who He is, He shows His way of doing things.

Through obedience, His people unlock His promises and the promises unlock the path to His kingdom and His kingdom to Him. God is *always* calling us to Him.

> Then I saw a new heaven and a new earth,
> for the first heaven and the first earth had
> passed away, and the sea was no more.
> And I saw the holy city, new Jerusalem,
> coming down out of heaven from God,
> prepared as a bride adorned for her hus-
> band. And I heard a loud voice from the
> throne saying, "Behold, the dwelling

place of God is with man. He will dwell
with them, and they will be his people,
and God himself will be with them as
their God. He will wipe away every tear
from their eyes, and death shall be no
more, neither shall there be mourning,
nor crying, nor pain anymore, for the
former things have passed away." And
he who was seated on the throne said,
"Behold, I am making all things new."
Also he said, "Write this down, for these
words are trustworthy and true." (Rev.
21:1–27)

You have to remember this also, for those that are in
Christ, we were transported from the kingdom of darkness
to the kingdom of everlasting light (kingdom of heaven). But
we're new immigrants there; we are learning the language and
learning the customs, and we still carry a lot of the mentality
of the kingdom we were born in. These are things that God
is working in us, in His way, to prepare us to operate in His
kingdom, to do our part for our new country, and to reap the
benefits of it too. None of that happens overnight.

When I first got to the United States from Cuba, I came
as a child. I picked up the language quickly and adapted
fairly quickly to the new environment. My mom, on the
other hand, lived most of her twenties in Cuba, her roots
ran deeper, and it took her longer to adapt. We all came to
this country with the promise of the American dream, a better life for our family, but achieving that dream required to
adapt new skills and customs to operate in this new country.
The promises of God work in a similar way; they call you to

His kingdom, and once there, there will be a growing and adapting process for them to manifest in your life.

They don't happen right away and won't happen without going through certain things that change you. There is a process to follow.

- The promises require a heart constantly aligned with God's.

Acts 8:9–24 talks about a magician who tried to buy from Peter the power of the Holy Spirit, so he too could heal the sick and give people the power of the Holy Spirit. What's more, the Bible says this man was also a believer and had been baptized. Peter's answer to the man:

> You have neither part nor lot in this matter, for your heart is not right before God. (Acts 8:21)

Manifesting the promises of God in your life require an involvement from the Holy Spirit and that requires a heart that is aligned with God's—wanting Him above anything He can give us, having a daily communion with Him every day, and working in the purposes that He has first. They work for others, and then they work for you.

God's heart is for you, as well as every other person living. He loves even those you do not know exist, and He saved you, as you asked Him to, but He also wants everyone else to be saved. So His promises are for you, as well as others; and the more you work toward His purposes, the more His promises will become active in your life, for the benefit of others watching you, as well as yours.

What Simon the Sorcerer failed to understand is this principle: there are no shortcuts with God. He saw the Holy Spirit as something that he could gain and make money with, but he did not take into account the person behind the Spirit. Peter answered correctly when he said he has no part in that matter. His heart wasn't aligned, so no power of the Holy Spirit could flow there.

• Grace before expectations.

There is only one instance I know where the promises of God manifest in people's lives that don't fit this mold, where a person who does not know God as deeply as they should activate promises in their lives that normally the would not be able to. I believe it's God's grace which allows for that to happen. He lifts the process so that person may receive benefits knowing that in doing so, that person will know Him better and will serve His purposes.

Before I was married, I lived with my girlfriend's parents while my father-in-law was going through cancer treatments. While my father-in-law grew up in church and had a relationship with God, my mother-in-law did not have as deep of a relationship. However, in that process, since starting to go to church, she dove deep believing in the promises of God for healing. Not knowing God as deeply as her husband, she shut down any doubt in her mind and believed in Him that He could do the miracle our family needed. To this day, we say that it was her faith that healed Robert from cancer. God allowed the promise of healing to come, responding to her faith.

The same could be said of the woman with the issue of blood in the Bible. She was a nameless stranger with a need, and she drew to Jesus knowing, somehow, that by reaching even the very edge of Him, she would be healed. This is a faith that reaches God in a violent way that unlocks the promises because it's a heart looking for His, believing beyond a shadow of a doubt, in who He is, and God rewards every sincere pursuit of Him.

> And a woman was there who had been subject to bleeding for twelve years. She had suffered a great deal under the care of many doctors and had spent all she had, yet instead of getting better she grew worse. When she heard about Jesus, she came up behind him in the crowd and touched his cloak, because she thought, "If I just touch his clothes, I will be healed." Immediately her bleeding stopped and she felt in her body that she was freed from her suffering.
>
> At once Jesus realized that power had gone out from him. He turned around in the crowd and asked, "Who touched my clothes?"
>
> "You see the people crowding against you," his disciples answered, "and yet you can ask, 'Who touched me?'"
>
> But Jesus kept looking around to see who had done it. Then the woman, knowing what had happened to her, came and fell at his feet and, trembling with fear, told him the whole truth. He said to her, "Daughter, your faith has healed you. Go in peace and be freed from your suffering." (Mark 5:25–34)

## The Process

There is something that we can tell ourselves when we're going through difficult circumstances, "This has limits." If you've ever flown in the window seat, you can see the ocean, islands, and cities beneath you. Then the plane goes through a cloud and you can't see anything but white and maybe some turbulence. Although that haze is all engulfing, it had a beginning, and it has an end; the plane eventually lands.

Likewise, although there will be times when we're in situations that consume everything around us, they were not always there, and they will not be there forever. Everything changes. The wisdom is being aware of these situations as pockets where your perception is distracted, where emotions run high because we are not ready to process them, and things are happening to you that you do not understand, but that eventually ends. We are being worked on by God, and the highest degree of trust is required.

> Trust in the LORD with all your heart and lean not on your own understanding; in all your ways submit to him, and he will make your paths straight. (Prov. 3:5–6)

God knows you, and He knows what you need. This quote from King Solomon has this implication—*our paths are not now straight.* Our way of processing is limited, and if we try to process situations by them, we'll arrive at the wrong conclusion. God is doing the work, and where reasoning fails, you must trust that He is good, and He is working to your benefit—whatever the optics look like.

Likewise, Jesus was teaching the crowds:

> So do not worry, saying, "What shall we eat?" or "What shall we drink?" or "What shall we wear?" For the pagans run after all these things, and your heavenly Father knows that you need them. But seek first his kingdom and his righteousness, and all these things will be given to you as well. (Matt. 6:31–33)

People focus on their needs, especially when their needs are about survival. And it's easy to let go of everything else and focus on the bare essentials, leaving God aside until we've resolved this issue or the other. What's more, Jesus says even God is aware of your needs and more so than you. So the solution that Jesus gives seems counterproductive, but in reality, it's exactly what the doctor ordered.

In your need, when you're knowing it and feeling it and creditors are calling your phone, you first look to align your heart with God and His system—His kingdom—not only will you get the solution to your problem, but you will also have more than you expected.

When you gain His kingdom and His righteousness, you become the kind of person that is able to operate in that kingdom. Jesus isn't offering a one-time solution to your problem. He isn't even offering a go-to solution every time you have a problem. He is effectively telling you that by doing what He tells you, you become the kind of person that not only never has to go through that problem again but will be in a constant growth to gain greater and greater ability! You will become the kind of person that instead of being in the hole, you throw the rope to pull someone else out of it.

He flips the situation on its head. Instead of becoming the person in need, you become the helper.

*It's all about the Holy Spirit.*

> So I say to you: Ask and it will be given to you; seek and you will find; knock and the door will be opened to you. For everyone who asks receives; the one who seeks finds; and to the one who knocks, the door will be opened. Which of you fathers, if your son asks for a fish, will give him a snake instead? Or if he asks for an egg, will give him a scorpion? If you then, though you are evil, know how to give good gifts to your children, how much more will your Father in heaven give the Holy Spirit to those who ask him! (Luke 11:9–13)

God is not ignorant of any part of your life. He knows your innermost thoughts, and He will work as far as you let Him. Accepting Jesus is the key and the start. This first act of faith allows God to come inside your heart. You now gain heaven and eternity. This is His grace.

But God is not done!

Then the Holy Spirit enters, and He is the constant connection between you and the Father. Through the Holy Spirit, the Father's will is known to you, and it's through the Holy Spirit that you get strength, wisdom, power, and endurance. Jesus opens the door on both sides—the door of heaven and the door of your heart. The Holy Spirit is the one that connects the two, carrying back and forth your prayers to the Father, interceding on your behalf, and counseling you on the Father and His business. He is the one that works inside of you.

This is the very best thing the Father can give you. Because not only do you get salvation, you also get access to the one thing that connects heaven and your heart. No matter what happens on earth, heaven is pouring into you and your heart. He is changing you from the inside out! *From the roots to the fruits!*

This isn't just a spiritual transformation or a change in circumstances that have no effect on the physical situation you're in—they work hand in hand. God transforms you, and through you, He transform the world around you. His kingdom come on everything your hand touches; and as He teaches you, and He transforms your inner man and your mind. You become the person He means you to be, and that person is far better than you can imagine for yourself!

If God gave you just the solution to your problem, you would be grateful and forgetful because nothing changed outside your circumstance. You would find yourself in a bigger problem down the line. There is a statistic showing that some of the people that win the lottery end up in a bigger financial hole than they were before winning. God gives you exactly what you need to not only resolve the problem you're in but to become the kind of person that problem never touches again and to help others through it.

## *Where Man and God Meet—the New Creation*

Remember, we were dead in our sins before God. Once God comes in, He starts with the heart but works outward to whatever you allow Him to work on. He has His own order of operating, and it's unique to every person. My process is different than yours, but God works in both of us. In that process, He will ask us to give Him parts of us we want to hold on to, anything that isn't the way He wants things to be.

It's a painful process and one we begrudgingly do until we know better.

But all our parts have to die, one by one, all of them have to die to us and be buried in surrender to Him.

> So is it with the resurrection of the dead.
> What is sown is perishable; what is raised
> is imperishable. (1 Cor. 15:42)

It's what God does with our dead parts that fills me with wonder. He does not lose any of them, but all of them will be raised again the way He meant them to be. Our dreams, hopes, gifts, relationships, everything—whatever God asks for, you give to Him, and He will give it back to you the way only He can.

> Beloved, we are God's children now, and
> what we will be has not yet appeared; but
> we know that when he appears we shall
> be like him, because we shall see him as
> he is. (1 John 3:2)

The more we give to God, the more He gives to us. The more we allow ourselves to be transformed into something more like Him. This process gets easier to go through when understanding that He is the one who is working. He is the one who transforms, and we trust in Him even when we don't understand anything.

But who we become will be something to marvel at.

> Do not marvel at this, for an hour is
> coming when all who are in the tombs
> will hear his voice. (John 5:28)

The savage mercies is that God allows pain, suffering, loss, and struggle to turn someone crooked and bent, who does not know any better, to be mended and be transformed into a citizen of the kingdom of heaven. You are reading this book because you've gone, are going, or will go through terrible things in life—welcome to the club.

I pray that you come to know God and trust Him above all things and to *never* take your eyes off Him. The world will try to distract you, but the One who overcame the world does not take His eyes off you. No matter what you go through, hold on to Him and let Him show you who He is and who you can be.

> Behold, it was for my welfare that I had great bitterness; but in love you have delivered my life from the pit of destruction, for you have cast all my sins behind your back. (Isa. 38:17)

Thank God for the savage mercies.

# about the author

Mauricio Crespo

At three years old, seeing his mother weeping because of their parents' divorce, Mauricio Crespo told her, "Mama, don't cry. My heart is yours." This sparked a passion for being present in a crisis. Graduating with a BS in psychology from Florida International University and Le Grande Diplome from Le Cordon Bleu, he uses his skills to help others go forward, whether they need a kind word, a good meal, or a swift kick in the rear.

He spends his free time cooking for his audacious nurse wife and tyrannical dachshunds.

# About Robert

At fifteen years old, Robert started his own construction business and since has built hundreds of custom homes in South Carolina and Florida. The fifth of six children, he mixes Southern love for family with a boyish sense of mischief, getting a rise out of everyone for a laugh, much to the chagrin of his wife.

Since overcoming stage 4 lung cancer that metastasized to seven different areas of his body, he readily tells anyone who will listen about the miracle God did in his life through the disease. Not only healing his body but also bringing his whole family to a deeper relationship with God and healing long-embedded rifts in his marriage. He lived the example that God, when trusted completely, can turn a tragedy into a blessing and is the only one who can.

He lived and died in Miami, Florida, surrounded by his family; and in his home, he entered heaven embraced by those that love him.